THE NEW BREED

PULPIT TO PAGE PUBLISHING CO. BOOKS MAY BE ORDERED THROUGH BOOKSELLERS OR BY CONTACTING:

PULPIT TO PAGE ‖ U.S.A & ABROAD

PULPITTOPAGE.COM

THE NEW BREED

THE RELEASE OF THE NEW WONDER-WORKING REFORMERS AND REVIVALISTS

BEN LIM

ENDORSEMENTS

Ben Lim is one of the most genuine hearts I have met in my time traveling as a worship leader and preacher. He is truly in love with Jesus and has met Him as a friend. As he shares his heart and life in this book you will encounter the reality of a living God in ways that you may have never experienced before. You will be challenged and encouraged as you are called into the place that God has ordained for you before the foundations of the world. Get ready to become a part of the *new breed*.

—JAKE HAMILTON,
Executive Director of Design and Culture
Stirring Church | Redding, CA

Ben Lim has done a masterful job in this book to give prophetic and practical insight into what God is doing in the earth, in this season of the Church. I believe that as we understand what God is doing, we can partner with heaven and propel Kingdom agendas. I applaud Ben for writing this book with such insight and clarity.

—ELIZABETH TIAM-FOOK,
Founder of International Young Prophets
Santa Rosa Beach, Florida

Ben Lim represents the rapidly-emerging next generation of prophetic voices to the Body of Christ in this fresh revelation called, *The New Breed*. The next generation is sometimes called the Elisha generation because we want our sons and daughters to have at least a double portion of everything we fought so hard for them to spiritually inherit. In *The New Breed*, Ben takes the reader to new levels of faith and expectation in all things good coming from the LORD. Now, writing of God operating on a newer, higher level, Ben says: "The visible world will be overcome by the spiritual. The waves, frequencies, and vibrations will be released through the voice of the Lord roaring out of your being. The Word in you will be amplified to levels and heights yet unknown and unheard." Don't miss your opportunity to be first-in-line to learn what God is prophesying over you. Young or old, if this book gets into your hand, you are part of *the new breed* yourself!

—STEVE SHULTZ,
Founder of The Elijah List

The New Breed will inspire you to step into the new move of God that is being unleashed on the earth. Get ready to be challenged to shift into the new as the *new breed* is Arising! Luke 5:38, "New wine must be poured into new wineskins."

—DAVID HERZOG,
thegloryzone.org | Scottsdale, Arizona

Ben Lim is a vibrant prophetic voice that burns with a fervent desire to see a new breed generation in the Church arise to carry God's glory to a hurting world. He combines a prophetic passion with the wisdom of apostolic grace to reveal a beautiful picture of what the church can do when it aligns with God's heart and principles. His inspirational approach will challenge you to a higher level and greater manifestation of God's power, love and glory and release a faith that you can change your life and your world!

—APOSTLE TOM HAMON,
Senior Pastor, Vision Church
Senior Leader, Christian International Apostolic Network

Ben Lim is a true new breed revivalist who is shaking the heavens and the earth. There is a fresh and passionate roar of victory that is being released from this dynamic man of God who walks in genuine signs, wonders, and miracles. This book is a true blueprint and manual for up and coming leaders that are committed to seeing the billion soul harvest that the Prophet Bob Jones prophesied about. Get what's in the book and get in the cloud of greater glory!

—REVIVALIST TODD BENTLEY,
President of Fresh Fire USA

Dr. Ben Lim carries a heart for revival and the presence of God's Spirit in this generation. He is a part of a new breed of revivalists who are committed to the guidance of the Word and empowering of the Holy Spirit. I believe this life-changing book will awaken in you a hunger for a manifestation of God's kingdom to come in your life, and then through your life. I highly recommend it!

—DR. ROBERT STEARNS,
Executive Director, Eagles' Wings
New York

The first time I met Ben Lim, I perceived the Grace of God over his life, and I immediately took an interest in him. He is certainly part of the New Breed that God is raising on this earth. The moment I read chapter 1 of this manuscript, I liked it immediately and it is evident that the grace I first saw in his life had grown substantially. Be blessed as you read this.

—REV. YANG TUCK YOONG,
Senior Pastor of Cornerstone Community Church
Singapore

In 2005, the Lord spoke to me that the church was entering a season of reformation. The reformation would be in our understanding of His Nature and Character. We need fearless voices to rise up in this hour with reformer's hearts to boldly proclaim what God is speaking to the church this hour. Ben Lim is one of those voices that represents *the new breed*. Ben carries both the crazy faith that marks this new breed as well as the humility to pointing to an authentic relationship with Jesus. I highly recommend this book to anyone looking to supercharge their faith.

—IVAN ROMAN,
Senior Leader of Empowered Life Church
Author of *Prophets Among Us*

Ben Lim is one of the voices God is raising up in this hour. He doesn't only preach with fire, but, he also writes with fire and this writing clearly demonstrates that. This is more than a book, this is an invitation into the lifestyle of the New Breed company! Get ready to find your new voice, receive a fresh fire, and be challenged to love with a fierce boldness. It's a new day! Be the New Breed!

—TONY KIM,
Senior Leader of Renaissance International
Founder & Director of Roar Collective/Online Academy
US National Director of Harvest International Ministry

The book you hold in your hand by Ben Lim entitled *The New Breed* has the power to change your life. It is filled with revelation and definition to what the Lord is releasing in our day. We have crossed the threshold of a new door in this season where a new breed of leader is beginning to come into view that will display new levels of the Glory of God. This Jesus People Generation is emerging with all of Heaven's DNA (Divine Nature Applied), and is being thrust into the nations as "glory dispensers" with astounding signs, wonders and miracles. The only language they understand, is what comes by waiting in the presence of the Holy Spirit. Meekness and humility are their trademark. The favor of God envelopes them, because of the anointing that rests on their lives. As harvesting machines, they will play a part in brining in the Billion Soul Harvest before the return of Jesus.

Look at what Isaiah wrote about them, "And He will lift up a signal to call together a fearless people from afar, and will hiss for them from the end of the earth [as bees are hissed from their hives], and behold, they shall come with speed, swiftly. None is weary or stumbles among them, none slumbers or sleeps; nor is the girdle of their loins loosed or the laces of their shoes broken; Their arrows are sharp, and all their bows bent; their horses' hoofs seem like flint, and their wheels like a whirlwind. Their roaring is like that of a lioness, they roar like young lions; they growl and seize their prey and carry it safely away, and there is none to deliver it." (Isaiah 5:28-29)

I highly recommend Ben's new book to all who hunger and thirst for more.

—JEFF JANSEN,
Global Fire Ministries International
Founder of Global Fire Church
Author of *Glory Rising, Furious Sound of Glory, Enthroned*

Ben Lim has captured the heart of God in this writing on the New Breed! This is a profound subject that I'm passionate about. It's absolutely necessary to accurately understand the season we are living in and the coming move of God. The new breeds will unlock new assignments, go on new adventures and dream new dreams. God is establishing the new breed to steward and release His Kingdom mandates in the earth. Read, enjoy and be equipped!

—RYAN LESTRANGE,
Author of #1 New Release *Hell's Toxic Trio*
Founder of RLM, TRIBE and iHubs Movement

Ben Lim is an emerging voice that God has raised up to connect the vintage faith to an emerging generation. His new book, *The New Breed* is strategically along those lines. Ben brings forth insight and revelatory truths that are sure to ignite passion and help equip the reader to be on the cutting edge of what the Lord is doing in this hour. Be prepared to be challenged and inspired to step into the new.

—SEAN SMITH,
Author of *Prophetic Evangelism* and *I Am Your Sign*
pointblankinternational.org
@revseansmith

Ben Lim is one of the most anointed and dedicated visionaries of our era. *The New Breed* directs the destiny and challenges this generation to lead the greatest revival before coming to Christ.

—DR. MICHELLE CORRAL,
Pastor, Author, and Teacher
Founder of Breath of the Spirit International Ministries

I want to dedicate this book to all of the raw, wild, and hungry radicals that are out there. The ones who are sold-out and the burning ones who want nothing but the more of God. We give you permission to be radical and to run after the Lord with all of your heart!

I also want to dedicate this book to the missionaries that have served and given their lives in the mission fields of the world. Thank you for your service and your fervor for the things of God. Thank you for serving into fulfilling the Great Commission.

CONTENTS

FOREWORD

THE LORD IS AT THE HEAD OF THE COLUMN
HE LEADS THEM WITH A SHOUT. THIS IS HIS
MIGHTY ARMY AND THEY FOLLOW HIS ORDERS.
THE DAY OF THE LORD IS AN AWESOME, TERRIBLE THING
WHO CAN POSSIBLY SURVIVE?

30 years ago, God gave me a prophetic word about an upcoming generation that would "change society and society would not change them." I believe that that generation is *here*. There is a new breed of people rising up from every nation and tribe with a fresh cry of revival in their hearts. They will not stop preaching the good news until everyone has heard and until they have all that the Bible has promised!

GOD BLESSES THOSE WHO WORK FOR PEACE
FOR THEY WILL BE CALLED THE CHILDREN OF GOD

They are the last day 'Army of the Lord' that the prophet Joel prophesied about (Joel 2:11). True sons of God (Matt. 5:9) are emerging in this hour and they are critical to the new thing that God is doing. Mike Bickle of IHOP Kansas City, once said that, "Twenty years from now, the Church will look completely different from what it looks like today." Like Mike Bickle, we believe that that prophecy is becoming a living reality today. For so long we have been crying out for a generation of young people who will carry the burden and the blessing of the double portion.

We believe that we are in a kairos season where that prayer is being answered. Ben Lim is one of those valiant, roaring voices whom the Lord is raising up, not just in signs and wonders, but in wisdom, honor, character, and holiness – the gifts of the Spirit married with the fruits of the Spirit. When a person desires nothing except God Himself, their hearts are aligned with His heart, so they will fully obey whatever He asks, no matter what the cost. Ben Lim is a man after God's own heart and his new book, *The New Breed* chronicles his own journey to become a person whose heart is fully obedient to the Word of God.

As you read this book, may you be marked with a fresh fire to become part of the new breed that the Prophet Bob Jones and many others have prophesied about. Our prayer for you is that this book causes revival to happen in your own heart first, and then in everyone you touch. So, not only do we recommend this book, but we also highly commend the man, Ben Lim. Receive God's message and messenger into your heart and be forever marked to become part of *The New Breed!*

—WESLEY AND STACEY CAMPBELL,
Founders of Be A Hero International
wesleystaceycampbell.com

A NOTE FROM THE AUTHOR

This book was birthed out of a twenty one day revival that we spontaneously had in our church in Los Angeles in the month of October to November 2017. That was such a tremendous and trying time in the Spirit. That was when I really learned to press into *the more* and learned what could happen when you begin to pay the price for an extended move of God.

The Lord met us every single day in such an unusual way with great signs and wonders. Each one of these chapters were prophetic words and decrees that were released as the days went by.

Not only is this book a prophetic word and revelation but it is an impartation of what we went through in that little underground basement church for twenty one days straight, crying out for the more of God.

The New Breed message came to me on the eighth day of this revival. The Lord began speaking to me about new beginnings and about being a new creation in Christ. And then the Lord began speaking to me that there is a new breed of people who will walk in the greatest dimension of signs, wonders, and miracles that the world has ever seen.

We are living in those times of limitless and endless possibilities. I pray that as you read this book, this impartation will grab a hold of you! Enjoy!

1

ELISHA GENERATION

When they had crossed, Elijah said to Elisha, "Tell me, what can I do for you before I am taken from you?" "Let me inherit a double portion of your spirit," Elisha replied. "You have asked a difficult thing," Elijah said, "yet if you see me when I am taken from you, it will be yours—otherwise, it will not."

As they were walking along and talking together, suddenly a chariot of fire and horses of fire appeared and separated the two of them, and Elijah went up to heaven in a whirlwind. Elisha saw this and cried out, "My father! My father! The chariots and horsemen of Israel!"

And Elisha saw him no more. Then he took hold of his garment and tore it in two. Elisha then picked up Elijah's cloak that had fallen from him and went back and stood on the bank of the Jordan. He took the cloak that had fallen from Elijah and struck the water with it.

"Where now is the Lord, the God of Elijah?" he asked. When he struck the water, it divided to the right and to the left, and he

crossed over. The company of the prophets from Jericho, who
were watching, said, "The spirit of Elijah is resting on Elisha."
And they went to meet him and bowed to the ground before him.
(2 Kings 9-15)

WHAT CAN I DO FOR YOU?

We are in a season where the Lord is asking us, "What
can I do for you?"

You are favored in the sight of God. You are His
favorite child. By grace, the Lord has brought us to a place before
Him where we have His utmost favor.

Jesus asked the blind man in Mark 10:51, "What do you want
me to do for you?" The blind man replied, "Rabbi, I want to see."

The mother of James and John came to Jesus and knelt down
to make a request. Jesus said, "What do you want?" (Matthew
20:21) Of course, as every good mother would, she said she wanted
Him to place her sons on the left and right of His throne.

The question of the hour is not what you can do for Jesus, but
what can Jesus do for you? What do you really believe God our
Father can do for you? Right now—in your family you're your
workplace, in your life?

DOUBLE-PORTION SONS

The word double comes from the Hebrew word shanah, which
means "double, repeated, duplicate, do it or speak it again for the
second time." All the great things You did in the life of Elijah, do
them again God! All the great things You did in the revivals of old!
Do it again God! All You did during the days of Azusa; do it again
God! Do it again and do it now!

Elijah was taken up right after crossing the Jordan. He released
a double portion of the Spirit of God on his life to his spiritual
son, Elisha. The Jordan River was where Jesus was baptized. This
was where Yeshua received the double portion of the Spirit of His

Father, YWH. As Elijah (his name meaning, "God is YWH") transferred a double-portion mantle to his son Elisha (his name meaning, "God is Salvation"), so it was once again, with the Father and Yeshua at the River Jordan hundreds of years later.

Jesus is releasing the greater anointing to do greater works. Jesus is baptizing us in the River Jordan so we can walk forward with a double portion of His mantle.

DOUBLE-RIVER PROPHETS

The Hebrew word for "prophet" in the Old Testament is nabi, which means "river." God is releasing a double portion of His river to flow out of the mouths of this generation. Elisha had twice what Elijah walked in. Which means he had double the mouth Elijah had. Not only should we have double the ears to hear, but we need to have double the mouths to speak God's Word. There will be such authority when we speak, that it'll feel and sound like God is speaking through us. It'll sound like the voice and strength of two people speaking through us.

God is raising up a generation that emanates and imitates the very voice of God. There are too many people making too much noise and saying too much nonsense. There are too many false and immature prophets. There are too many people proclaiming that they are prophesying in God's name when there is no weight to what they are saying. God is moving us from being a noisy people of clanging gongs and cymbals, to a people of harmonious praise and worship.

Even in the Church, people are like horses who need to have their tongues and mouths bridled with something. The Holy Spirit will train us how and what to speak.

I will instruct you and teach you in the way you should go; I will counsel you with my loving eye on you. Do not be like the horse or the mule, which have no understanding but must be controlled by bit and bridle or they will not come to you. (Psalm 32:8-19)

The Lord doesn't want to control us. In fact, His love is so great, strong, secure, that He doesn't need to control us. He is that confident in Himself and in His great, selfless, unending love. He is confident in this overcoming love relationship between Himself and His Bride.

The Lord doesn't want to control us. That is witchcraft and going against our will. We are not slaves and servant-beings that must do His every bidding. We have a choice. We have been gifted with the ultimate God-like quality, which is to have free will. The Lord wants us to choose to hear Him, follow Him, and to go in the way of His loving eye. It's all about love.

That word eye, in the Greek, is the same word as the word for the eyes that cover the bodies of the four living creatures around the throne of God. Each of the four living creatures had six wings and was covered with eyes all around, even under its wings. Day and night they never stop saying: 'Holy, holy, holy is the Lord God Almighty,' who was, and is, and is to come. (Revelation 4:8)

The Lord is the all-knowing, all-seeing, omnipotent, omnipresent, omniscient God. He is everywhere and He sees and knows all things. Nothing is hidden from the eyes of God, which surround and cover the four living creatures, which prophetically symbolize the four characters of God.

His loving eye is on you. You are the apple of His eye. He wants to lead you by His perfect, prophetic vision. He wants to lead you with love and instruction; by being lost in the gaze of His eyes. By having deep and direct, unbroken eye contacts; eyes locked together, in love. He wants us to see as He sees. He wants us to move as He moves. The Lord is breaking us free from every limiting system. Nothing can control love. Nothing can put a lid on love. The Lord will lead you in the way of love, with great direction, through deep love connection.

He is giving you His sight. The precious eye of the eagle is upon you. He knows all things and He sees all things. Walk with Him into victory and the path of the dawn. The Lord wants us to be prophets, people of His spoken, written, and manifested Word.

The Lord wants us to be a people who know how to hear the words of His mouth and to walk out the words from our mouths. If there is a sword in the mouth of Jesus, then what's in yours? (Revelation 19:15)

Jesus told His disciples not to worry about what they would say or do when they were brought before kings, governors, and rulers. The Holy Spirit would speak through them. The Holy Spirit also will anoint your mouth to utter the mysteries of Christ to all who hear, near and far. Your voice will be so anointed that people will wake up from their sleep with fear and trembling. Your voice will be so anointed that people miles away will hear what the Lord is speaking. Your voice will be so anointed that there will be no need for sound systems, microphones, or electronics. The visible world will be overcome by the spiritual. The waves, frequencies, and vibrations will be released through the voice of the Lord roaring out of your being. The Word in you will be amplified to levels and heights yet unknown and unheard.

Out of the mouth of babes and nursing infants You have ordained strength, Because of Your enemies, That You may silence the enemy and the avenger." (Psalm 8:2 NKJV)

Literally, babies will come out of their mothers's wombs proclaiming the Word of the Lord. Children of all ages will declare of the glory of God in schools and public places, and it will be broadcast on international media and television. We are in the days when the Holy Spirit is anointing His children to do great and mighty signs and wonders.

The innocence of children's simple faith is greater than the wiles of the enemy. God is calling out the children. God is calling out the teenagers. God is calling both young and old to take a stand to live radically normal lives. We are entering a time when youth and children are going to spring up with power, passion, and purity, having no form of defilement in them—like Daniel and his friends.

In a day when pornography, video games, social media, and other forms of idolatrous distraction are sweeping the earth, the Lord is raising up a pure breed, a new breed with a Kingdom mandate. These children will be devoted unto the Lord from birth. They will testify of the Lord straight from their mother's wombs. These children will utter and prophesy things that have never been heard! These children of the new breed will walk in a different Spirit—His Holy Spirit.

ELISHA GENERATION

The Elisha generation will fulfill the dreams of their Elijah fathers. The Elisha generation will see the death of Jezebel. Our fathers and mothers have dreamed of many things, but unfortunately most of them remained mere dreams. This isn't bad or shameful, but presents a hopeful opportunity for us, the Elisha Generation. This is a hope-filled opportunity for those who understand the ripeness of the times. We are the new breed! We will walk in the promises and prophecies are forefathers dreamed of, toiled, and interceded for in past generations. The time is now to see the bowls of incense in the Heavens above tip over and pour out all across the earth.

We will be a generation that comes out of the birthing canal unharmed, undeterred, unscathed, and undefiled. There is so much hurt, wounding, division and battle scars that our parents had to go through that we aren't able to understand. However, none of it is coincidence; it is for great Kingdom purposes. There is a generation rising out of the ashes of their forefathers' shame, sadness, victories, and triumphs. This generation will not need to go through the same junk and gunk that our parents went through. The sins of the fathers will not found in the children. The children will move forth in righteousness and purity their parents only dreamed of and gave their lives for.

Many will say, "My ears have heard of you, but now my eyes

have seen!" The days of the shadow are deteriorating and diminishing so that there is only light.

This generation will move in so much more than our fathers and mothers walked in because the battles our parents fought have won complete purity for us to start from. We will know the glory, and not just in part. We will only experience Jesus, not idolize the exaltation of another man, woman, or minister. It is not because we choose to parade ourselves above our fathers and mothers, but because we've humbled ourselves in such a way that their ceiling becomes our floor. Because of the prayers and love of our Elijah fathers and mothers, we shall be birthed out with great dunamis power as the Elisha Generation.

GOD IS MY SALVATION!

Many people have talked about the Spirit of Elijah, and how the John the Baptists are preparing the way. This is absolutely necessary and important. However, the Lord is raising up the Elisha generation, meaning, "the Lord is Savior!"

The Elisha generation will see the salvation of their God! There will be not only a preparation but the manifestations of promises! There won't only be training, but deliverances for the people of God! There will be the raising of the dead! There will be the multiplication of food, supply, and provision. There will be great power released in the heavens and the earth because of this Elisha Generation who believe that today is the day of salvation.

And most importantly, the spirit of Jezebel will be defeated! The spirit of Jezebel will no longer contend with the Spirit of Elijah. The spirit of Baal can longer contend with the Spirit of Hashem, YWH. The false prophets will no longer be any match for the prophets of God. The seductive, manipulative, controlling spirit of Jezebel will no longer be tolerated! There is a holy remnant of 7,000 that have not bowed their knees to Baal! There is a perfected remnant that has kept themselves holy unto the Lord for such a time as this. The spirit of Jezebel will be defeated! Different Jeze-belic types of figures will no longer exist in our church circles and in the different spheres of society because the Elisha generation, the double-portion sons, will rise up with such power, authority, and integrity, that they will see their fathers' and mothers' adversary defeated once and for all. The tests and tribulations of their parents will not be transferred down into the lives of their children.

CHARACTERISTICS OF THE JEZEBEL SPIRIT:

- Controlling (seeks to control authority and leaders at the highest levels) (1 Kings 21:4-17)
- Manipulative (1 Kings 21:4-17)
- Condemnatory (1 Kings 21:4-17)
- Scares prophets (1 Kings 19:2-3)
- Kills the prophetic move (1 Kings 18:4,19:2-3)
- Kills the future, the next move of God (abortions, innocent blood shed) (1 Kings 18:4, 18:13)
- Preys on the weak (2 Kings 19:2-3)
- Seductive and sensual (2 Kings 9:30, Revelation 2:20)
- Enforces and institutes false worship (1 Kings 16:31-34, 18:18-19)

CHARACTERISTICS OF THE ELISHA SPIRIT:

- Honors fathers and mothers (1 Kings 2:19)
- Generous and humble (1 Kings 2:21)
- Double-portion inheritance (2 Kings 2:9)
- Faithful and loyal (2 Kings 2:2)
- Hungry for the miraculous (2 Kings 2:14)
- Good stewards (2 Kings 2:13)
- Loves and serves the one (2 Kings 4:1-7, 8-37, 42-44, 5:1-19)

THE LATTER GLORY

The LORD restored the fortunes of Job when he prayed for his friends, and the LORD increased all that Job had twofold. (Job 42:10)

This two-fold, double-portion anointing rested on our patriarch, Job, who suffered much. His faith in the Lord was tried in every way and from every angle. However, the Lord blessed Job in the latter part of his life.

After Job had prayed for his friends, the Lord restored his fortunes and gave him twice as much as he had before. All his brothers and sisters and everyone who had known him before came and ate with him in his house. They comforted and consoled him over all the trouble the Lord had brought on him, and each one gave him a piece of silver and a gold ring.

The Lord blessed the latter part of Job's life more than the former part. He had fourteen thousand sheep, six thousand camels, a thousand yoke of oxen and a thousand donkeys. And he also had seven sons and three daughters. The first daughter he named Jemimah, the second Keziah and the third Keren-Happuch. Nowhere in all the land were there found women as beautiful as Job's daughters, and their father granted them an inheritance along with their brothers.

After this, Job lived a hundred and forty years; he saw his children and their children to the fourth generation. And so Job died, an old man and full of years. (Job 42:10-17)

How would you like it if the Lord blessed the latter part of your life more than the former? The last is surely the first! He has saved the best wine for last (John 2:10)! Job's restoration consisted of great prosperity, provision, prominence, long life, and a good name. These are all fruits birthed from the fear of the Lord.

The latter part of Job's life was greater, more prosperous, and more renowned than the first part. But it wasn't easy. He paid a price. It cost him greatly, but it was well worth it. You may not know what is at the end of your current trial and situation, but it most certainly is victory and assured spoils and glory. The momentary crown of thorns will disappear and turn into an eternal crown of glory. The momentary trials and tribulations will produce a mature Bride. The momentary tears will turn into momentous celebrations and years unending of heavenly bliss.

There was no comparison between the first and second parts of Job's life. This is the same revelation found in the power of the first Adam compared to Jesus, the second Adam.

The floods of God's grace covered the past life of Job, leaving no trace, just as the floods of Noah's time covered and removed all that was known! There was only newness of life; a new beginning; a new start! That's what the blood of Jesus does. It doesn't just cover the past—it completely removes it by magnifying God's infinite goodness, grace, and mercy. The past is buried so deeply under the great layers of love that it becomes obsolete and nearly blotted out from all memory. That's what the blood of Jesus does; it completely removes all sin and death.

The days to come will be filled with greater glory. The wealth of the nations as recorded in Exodus 12:35-36 will be handed to us as we move into greater glory from our days of Egypt into the promised land.

We will be sent out with the gold, the wealth, the riches of the nations. However, don't turn it into an idol. Don't put your past up on a pedestal. Look unto King Jesus, the Alpha and the Omega, Who forever sits on the throne.

When you forget how far the Lord has brought you during your journey through the wilderness, remember the items of gold that were given to you. Remember the objects of redemption in your life. Remember the things that have been rightly returned to you in restitution for all that belongs to you.

———

THE MANTLES

There are many mantles up for grabs. The mantles of people like Kathryn Kuhlman, Aimee Semple McPherson, John Alexander Dowie, William Branham, John G. Lake, Bill Bright, Bob Jones, and even the late Kim Clement.

The great cloud of witnesses worked tirelessly and travailed greatly so we wouldn't need to labor as they did. They did so out of their obedience to the Lord, knowing their lives and mantles would be batons pushed forward into the hands of the next runners and winners of this generation.

Hunger and honor are the ways we receive these mantles. We won't be able to fully receive a thing if we don't know that it exists; therefore, studying revival history is extremely important. Knowing the history of our genealogy in Christ is a given when we walk out our sonship. Being a son means we are aware of our Father's heart and our family's history. Being a son can be defined as "walking in the awareness of the Great Cloud of Witnesses."

Not only should we be aware of the Great Cloud of Witnesses, but we should also learn to partner with them. In truth, we are all connected in the Spirit with those who have gone before us. These mantles can be physical, tangible things; clothing, anointing oil, a watch, anything! The anointing can be transferred through anything.

TRANSFERENCE OF MANTLES

- Peter's shadow healed the sick. (Acts 5:15)
- Paul's aprons and handkerchiefs healed the sick. (Acts 19:12)
- Elijah dropped his mantle to Elisha. (2 Kings 2:14)
- There was still power in the bones of Elijah's tomb. (2 Kings 13:21)

I believe these mantles can be retrieved and received in the

Spirit, but also can be transferred through tangible, physical items. God can do anything and many times, He has a way of confounding the thoughts of men.

Mantles are the outer robes that are worn and seen by all men. They are the fruits born from the roots on the inside, intertwined with the Root of David. The fruit of our lives is the mantle we carry and walk around in. Every school has its own type of mantle. Every tribe has its own. Every family has its own kind of symbol. In olden times you would know if someone was royalty or a common shepherd. The mantle wasn't just physical clothes, but the spirit man manifesting itself through all a person was. It was their aura, shining bright light and colors or dim, dark gloominess. It's important to learn to joyfully try on our fathers' mantles. That is how we can learn to walk as they did. The Bible says Solomon walked in the ways of his father, David. Solomon showed his love for the Lord by walking according to the instructions given him by David, except that he offered sacrifices and burned incense on the high places. (1 Kings 3:3) He still had false worship in his heart.

Proverbs says:

Listen, my son, to your father's instruction and do not forsake your mother's teaching. They are a garland to grace your head and a chain to adorn your neck. (Proverbs 1:8-9)

There are mantles the Lord wants us to adorn us with. Without them, we may stray far away from the examples the Lord's placed in our lives.

The mantles of the Great Cloud of Witnesses—those who are now in the Great Hall of Fame and Faith, as recorded in Hebrews 11—are transferrable. These mantles are, in a sense, the giftings and anointings a person has received and achieved. These Heavenly inheritances should not be wasted. These mantles are waiting for the right people to receive them and take them up to the next level.

These mantles are waiting to be dug up and properly transferred from generation to generation. They belonged are generals who plowed tremendous things in the Spirit and in the natural. These are destinies waiting to become linked with our stories and genealogies, but many of us don't receive or experience the fullness of our inheritance because of complacency, ignorance, and/or pride. We need Holy Ghost activations of all such inheritances, which come through the walk of life.

The devil doesn't want us to be aware of what is available to us, or pass those things on to the next generation. The devil doesn't want us to receive our inheritance. The enemy wants to stop the line of unity and block the flow of the Spirit.

These inheritances are crying out for us to pick them up and move forward in greater capacities than the previous generation.

"Very truly I tell you, whoever believes in me will do the works I have been doing, and they will do even greater things than these, because I am going to the Father." (John 14:12)

The Lord has commissioned us to do greater things because His Spirit is within us. He has transferred all that He has and is into us. Be like Jesus. Walk out His mantle. Walk out the mantles of old. Receive the full inheritance of your salvation and of our Kingdom.

"And if the Spirit of him who raised Jesus from the dead is living in you ..." (Romans 8:11)

"As for you, the anointing you received from him remains in you, and you do not need anyone to teach you. But as his anointing teaches you about all things and as that anointing is real, not counterfeit—just as it has taught you, remain in him." (1 John 2:27)

———

TEAR THE OLD, WEAR THE NEW

Elisha saw this and cried out, "My father! My father! The chariots and horsemen of Israel!" And Elisha saw him no more. Then he took hold of his garment and tore it in two.

Elisha then picked up Elijah's cloak that had fallen from him and went back and stood on the bank of the Jordan. He took the cloak that had fallen from Elijah and struck the water with it. "Where now is the Lord, the God of Elijah?" he asked. When he struck the water, it divided to the right and to the left, and he crossed over. (2 Kings 2:12-14)

The power of the mantle was evident and was apparently active and available. However, it was now time for Elisha to begin to walk out his maturity and sonship in wearing the heavy robes of his father. It was time for him to grow to fit into his father's shoes. Eventually, he would outgrow the shoes, the mantle, and the ministry of his father. This is Kingdom succession. This is Kingdom transference. This is a double-portion son.

The Bible says Elisha first tore his own clothes. This is interesting. He tore in two the very garment he had. He was pretty much naked now, probably left in his undergarments.

From there, he took the physical, tangible mantle of Elijah, and the anointing and power of God manifested from it. I believe Elisha clothed himself with it. He wore his father's mantle for however many days to come. Elisha preserved what was most precious to him, which was the mantle of his father Elijah. It wasn't just a spiritual mantle, but there was something dear and true in the physical. I believe Elisha wore it like his own, proudly, thinking about his father Elijah, and even feeling like his great hero.

Sometimes we need to rip apart the old. In order to wear the new, we must sometimes tear away from the old. It doesn't matter how comfortable and used to the old we've become, there are new levels and mantles that the Lord wants us to wear and to war in.

As Elijah asked Elisha, and as Jesus asked the blind men, "What do you want me to do for you?" What do you want the Lord to do for you? Do you believe that you are a double-portion son and you can boldly ask the Father for the desires of your heart before the throne of grace? Ask away. Ask away for the more of God. Be the Elisha generation that the world has been waiting for.

THE NEW BREED

Therefore if anyone is in Christ, he is a new creature; the old things passed away; behold, new things have come.
(2 Corinthians 5:17)

There is a new generation rising that the world has never seen before. They will be walking in such heavenly Kingdom technology, that the fallen angels and all their demonic technology won't be able to compete with it. All of the old has passed away and the new continues on!

NEW BEGINNINGS

God is into new beginnings. Over and over again, the Bible records numerous accounts, of God starting afresh with His nation, Israel. The Bible is filled with examples of God's good and perfect nature, the God of the second chances. He loves making all things new! He's taking us from glory to glory, which means we will constantly be entering into realms and mysteries that have yet to unfold. Searching out the wonders of God and experiencing His heavenly bliss will never get old. The things of God are infinite, unlimited, and always abounding! We are strapped to Him, flying high in the ride of our lives! We are still at the beginning of the beginning.

The true Gospel is rarely taught these days. The Gospel of the Kingdom was all that Jesus preached about and demonstrated. He didn't just talk about it, He walked it out. It was the realm He lived in and from. The Good News is still good news, and the Lord is bringing us into greater fascination with the simplicity of the beauteous Gospel. Simple yet supernatural. Simple yet profound. Simple yet powerful. The Lord is causing us to fall in love with Him, being with Him, and the wondrous things of His heart.

The Lord is raising up a new breed has never been seen before. They are a breed of people that has been seen in part but will surprise everyone! They will even surprise the angels of Heaven and the Great Cloud of Witnesses. The ancient angels have been waiting to partner with such a radical, yet normal breed of believers. They will believe in the whole Word of God and believe in it for today! It's not good theology if it cannot be experienced.

This new breed will walk out their true born-again nature. They will not waste time with the religious mumbo-jumbo of the Church, but will truly understand what it means to be a new creation.

A NEW HEART IS A NEW START

And I will give them one heart, and put a new spirit within them And I will take the heart of stone out of their flesh and give them a heart of flesh. (Ezekiel 11:19)

On the contrary, a person is a Jew who is one inwardly, and circumcision is of the heart—by the Spirit, not the letter. That man's praise is not from men but from God. (Romans 2:29) There is a new beginning that is dawning on the sons of the Church. There is a new beginning that is being cut into the fabric of our future.

The number eight in Hebrew stands for new beginnings. It was on the eighth day after birth that Hebrew boys were circumcised. The circumcision stood for making a covenant with God. It stood for all of their offspring becoming one in the blood covenant with Jesus. It stood for giving their bodies to the Lord. As Jesus was marked on His body in establishing the New Covenant, the men of Israel were also circumcised, signifying the marking of the new covenant.

The foreskin of the flesh was cut off. God is cutting off the excess and the works of the flesh. He is cutting off the old, dead man. He is cutting off the sinful nature. He is cutting us off from our past, addictions, habits, and the things that used to chain and bind us. The Lord has cut us from the ways of the world and delivered us to Himself. The Lord has covenanted with us in marriage, as a holy union between Heaven and earth, God and man.

Allow the Lord to cut off the old! Allow Him to prune the things that came between you and Him. This generation will eagerly desire to have all negativity cut away from their lives. They will throw themselves to the truth and grab hold of what is real. They will fly away from what is fake, false, and fleeting, and will be caught up into what is real, authentic, and God-made, not man-made. They will cut themselves away from the counterfeit.

The Lord is circumcising death away from our hearts. He is truly empowering us to feel and to be. He has cut off all the ties we may have made, knowingly or unknowingly, with the devil. He is cutting off all unholy soul ties, and they are now nailed to the cross! All the things that have been cut from us are now dead, buried and forever finished. They no longer exist, as wrath has been poured out against it.

God is in the business of checking our hearts. He is circumcising the measures and motives of who we are and all we do. He desires hearts of purity; men and women who have singleness of heart and vision. People who are not swayed in their bodies, souls, or spirits. People who look distinctly different from the rest of the world.

HEART CIRCUMCISION

"The LORD your God will circumcise your hearts and the hearts of your descendants, so that you may love him with all your heart and with all your soul, and live." (Deuteronomy 30:6)

There is excruciating pain in circumcision. There was no pain medicine or modern technology in ancient Israel like we have today. There were only flint knives in the hands of holy and anointed, God-fearing ministers. The pain was supposed to be felt because the marking in the body was meant to be remembered. Many times, the Lord speaks loudest and reveals Himself the most in times of pain, trial, and tribulation. There is a great revelation of love and grace over the circumcision of our hearts.

It is only by cutting the umbilical cord that ties you to your mother at birth that you can begin to fully function on your own and begin to produce the oxygen and nutrients your little baby body needs! The Lord wants us to begin to mature by being able to produce the nutrients from Him, and to become strong in Him.

These knives, these swords of the Spirit, are the only thing that can cut off the dead skin that slimed us from the Fall of Man. That slithering, cold nature of the serpent has now been cut away. We are now as smooth and soft as the skin of the sacrificed Lamb!

A heart circumcision represents being made a new creation. We don't have the Holy Spirit living in us so we can be swayed by the old passions of the flesh. The Holy Spirit is in us to grant us victory and greater glory, not continual defeat and loss! The Holy Spirit is in us because He's committed to see us walk out our Christ identity in the new covenant. He wants us to move forward into places we've never been before, not stay stuck and comfortable in what is known. When our hearts are circumcised, we become new. Heart circumcision is the essential core of the new breed.

The issues of life flow from the heart. (Proverbs 4:23) God

wants us to take care of our hearts. He doesn't just want us to have His new heart, but He wants us to take care of our own.

He wants us to have new hearts, not just theologically, but to practically see our new hearts fully alive, emotionally and spiritually. It is important that our hearts feel as alive as His heart is. The sole purpose of our existence is so our hearts feel the eternal life and love of God.

HEART OF LOVE

This new breed will understand what it means to be a new creation. They will understand what it means to walk out the resurrected nature of Christ. Christ will be their identity. Christ crucified will be all they know. They will fully walk out all Christ has for them. The greater things will be done in Jesus' name! "Feel love, be love, do love, and think love!"

He answered, "'Love the Lord your God with all your heart and with all your soul and with all your strength and with all your mind'; and, 'Love your neighbor as yourself.'" (Luke 10:27)

God wants us to feel His love and compassion at all times. Feel the love. Feel His love for all mankind.

LOVE IS AUTHENTIC

This generation is dying for the authentic. As the Millennial generation is flooded with information, noise, distractions, and clutter, they are starving for a true connection.

The Lord said to Moses and Aaron, "When Pharaoh says to you, 'Perform a miracle,' then say to Aaron, 'Take your staff and throw it down before Pharaoh,' and it will become a snake." So Moses and Aaron went to Pharaoh and did just as the Lord commanded. Aaron threw his staff down in front of Pharaoh and his officials,

and it became a snake. Pharaoh then summoned wise men and sorcerers, and the Egyptian magicians also did the same things by their secret arts: Each one threw down his staff and it became a snake. But Aaron's staff swallowed up their staffs. Yet Pharaoh's heart became hard and he would not listen to them, just as the Lord had said. (Exodus 7:8-13)

The Lord commissioned Moses to go up to Pharaoh and to declare that the God of Israel wantedHis people back. The heart of this was so they would return to worship Him. Worship was at the core of this great deliverance. Worship is at the center of a circumcised heart.

Moses went up with Aaron's staff. This was an everyday, average item—but it would be transformed and used for something historic and miraculous in the Lord's name.

Don't neglect the mundane. Don't neglect the simple. Don't neglect the things that may seem not-so-spiritual or holy. God can and will use all things! He is not limited by things that don't fit into our box of understanding. He will take the natural and turn it into the supernatural.

The most famous and powerful magicians and sorcerers of the day mocked the God of Israel when Aaron's rod turned into a snake. They mocked Moses and bragged that they could do this little trick with their own demonic powers. Lo and behold, the staff in Moses' hand ate up the other snakes of the magicians. Nothing can come against the power of God. Nothing can come against the supernatural touch of the Gospel.

The authentic will always swallow up the shallow, the superficial and the counterfeit. The new breed will be all about authenticity. The new breed will be all about manifesting weighty truth rather than hype and excitement. The new breed will be all for seeing Christ glorified. They will hunger for the truth rather than mere facts. They will spend themselves to see all that Jesus is become true in their day and generation.

THE NEW BREED

The new breed will walk in a new way that is totally different from the greats of old. God is doing a new thing and it isn't church as usual. The Church will never be the same again. We are entering a new move of God, when the days of old will be fully eclipsed by the tsunami wave of glory, miracles, and souls untold!

Don't be like the Israelites who kept sticking to the ways of Egypt, grumbling and complaining. Don't be like those who perished in the desert because of their unbelief. Don't be like those didn't walk into the new because they continued to walk out the old ways of proud and unrepentant hearts. Stop looking back to the old days of Egypt. Look forward to the new days of Israel. Stop looking back to the old days of glory. Start looking forward to the greater days of guts and glory.

Stop comparing the present to the past. It's important to look to the past to remember how far the Lord's brought us. The Bible and the Old Testament is filled with commandments from the Lord to remember the past; however, don't stay there.

Stay present and look to the future. The Lord wants us to give our attention to the foresight of Christ, not just the hindsight. He wants us to have vision for the future, not just the past. He wants us to move forward into new and greater breakthroughs, not to stay stuck in the victories of yesterday.

It's important to honor the past moves of God but don't idolize them. It's important to honor our fathers and mothers, but they are not our god. God wants us to move into the new thing. What does it look like? Who knows? We all see in part and know in part, but I don't think anybody has the full picture. We are in a new era in which the Lord is increasingly surprising the Bride with new wisdom and insight.

Many people have stated that it's going to be like the days of Azusa, or Aimee Semple McPherson, or like the days of the Moravians. I believe all these past moves of God were necessary and vital, but they were not the absolute picture of what the Lord is doing and wants to do. They serve as examples for what is to come. They are shadows becoming substance.

"These things happened to them as examples and were written down as warnings for us, on whom the culmination of the ages has come." (1 Corinthians 10:11)

THE NEW MOVE

The new thing looks like you and me. The move the Lord is manifesting across the earth comes in the package of you and me. God is moving in such a way that it takes your true you to come to life. It takes your true you to be a part of it.

I believe the new thing is not repeating the past, but taking the best of what's been done and truly stepping forward on these platforms and floors of what were once ceilings and heights. We will move forward from the shoulders of our fathers.

"For behold, I create new heavens and a new earth; and the former things will not be remembered or come to mind." (Isaiah 65:17)

The former things will no longer be remembered. There is a new breed rising with resurrection power, creative knowledge, and freedom that the world has never seen. There is a new breed that will rule and reign from the new heavens and the new earth. This new breed will emanate the love and perfection of the New Jerusalem.

If it's in Jesus, then it's in you. If it's not in Jesus, then it's not in you. This the full definition of the new breed. The new breed is the now breed.

3

GOVERNMENT OF JUSTICE

Taking dominion is not just a theological mindset or belief. It is an actuality. All things are under our feet. We can take control and shift the atmosphere in the Spirit. We can discern what is needed most and release it to shift our surroundings.

The government of Heaven is established on the shoulders of men and women who have surrendered themselves to the Lord. The ekklessia is assembling and advancing today in every sphere of society.

The Lord loves to use average men and women to expand His Kingdom. We are His gateway, His portal. If Christ the door is inside of us, that also makes us doors. Not only are we ambassadors of the Kingdom, but we are gatekeepers and point of contacts for the Kingdom to be released.

A LIFE OF JUSTICE

He has shown you, O mortal, what is good. And what does the LORD require of you? To act justly and to love mercy and to walk humbly with your God. (Micah 6:8)

Acting justly means to act out the Law of Heaven. to properly act as a law-giver, judge, or governor. The Lord wants us to be His people, who act like Him. The Lord wants us to live a life of justice. Justice happens when Jesus happens. The Bible says that the nations will be drawn to the light of our justice.

Here is my servant, whom I uphold, my chosen one in whom I delight; I will put my Spirit on him, and he will bring justice to the nations. (Isaiah 42:1)

"Arise, shine, for your light has come, and the glory of the Lord rises upon you. See, darkness covers the earth and thick darkness is over the peoples, but the Lord rises upon you and his glory appears over you. Nations will come to your light, and kings to the brightness of your dawn. "Lift up your eyes and look about you: All assemble and come to you; your sons come from afar, and your daughters are carried on the hip. Then you will look and be radiant, your heart will throb and swell with joy; the wealth on the seas will be brought to you, to you the riches of the nations will come. Herds of camels will cover your land, young camels of Midian and Ephah. And all from Sheba will come, bearing gold and incense and proclaiming the praise of the Lord. All Kedar's flocks will be gathered to you, the rams of Nebaioth will serve you; they will be accepted as offerings on my altar, and I will adorn my glorious temple. (Isaiah 60:1-7)

Nations will come to our light in the times of darkness and shadows. Nations will come to you for answers, for vision, for assurance, for hope, for revelation, and for clarity. Nations will come to you because of the favor of the Lord rising upon you. But first, we must arise.

Our prime responsibility in shining our light is in rising. We must rise up and above the ashes, the norms of the day, and from the ways of the world. We must rise up and above the things that try to hold us down and define and defy us.

There will be a flood of people coming to seek your counsel. There will be a flood of people coming to be fed from the bowl of your wisdom, just as the Queen of Sheba sought out King Solomon. There will be a flood of people who will look to you as their spiritual father and mother, as their leader and covering.

There also will be a transference of wealth! The wealth of the nations will come to you. There will be no hindrance to the flow of resources. The nations will trust you with their riches. They will put their trust in you as you rise up in the Lord's anointing with wisdom and integrity. The nations will come to you with the best of their fortunes and give them to you.

The nations will come to your light as they did with Joseph. In times of famine, calamity, and darkness, the dignitaries and leaders of all peoples will come to you for wisdom, help, and health. All this is for the adorning of His holy temple. The light of justice that shines and burns brightly will be the menorah, which is at the center of the temple of God. All of this is for the building of the house of worship for our God.

SPIRIT OF JUBILEE

The Spirit of the Sovereign Lord resting upon us is for the sake of justice! For setting the captives free and for proclaiming the year of the Lord's favor! The Lord is making every wrong thing right. The Lord is sending His truth and mercy from the court-rooms of Heaven. The Lord is decreeing a thing and it shall come to pass.

People being sick is not right. Children being abandoned and orphaned is not right. Skyrocketing divorce rates are not right. People starving in Third World nations is not right. The unborn being murdered is not right. There are many things in this fallen world that are not right. However, the Lord wants to make all these things right and restore them to an even greater level than their original design and purpose.

The world cannot be restored to its righteous ordination until it fully receives the manifestation of God's sons. The world has been waiting for the judgment of the final settlement on Calvary. It has been settled and the verdict has been won! Christ has won! The rugged cross of Calvary has become the final testament of the world returning to its original glory and righteousness in its Creator. Joy to the world, for the Lord has come!

Just then, an angel of the Lord stood before them, and the glory of the Lord shone around them, and they were terrified. But the angel said to them, "Do not be afraid! For behold, I bring you good news of great joy that will be for all the people."
(Luke 2:9-10)

The world has been waiting for its Savior to come! The Savior of the world, who would liberate all of creation from bondage, came in the form of an infant child. The world would return to its original stature through the life of a human being; fully God, yet fully man.

God wants to release heavenly Kingdom justice through human beings who walk in the fear of God. God wants to release Kingdom justice not just in the areas of need, but in the areas of His leading. There is so much that needs the touch of God. Be what the world's been waiting for. Be what all of creation has been longing for; a righteous son, walking in Kingdom justice.

Wherever you walk, the land will be given to you. The Lord wants us to be priests who walk to and fro, all throughout the land, gaining the rightful territory that belongs to us. This is part of the Spirit of Jubilee. All the land, animals, and possessions that rightfully belong to you will be returned. We are living in the days of Jubilee! We are living in the days of restoration and restitution. We are living in the days of the seven-fold return and increase.

HEAVENLY WISDOM

The Lord wants to give us wisdom as we handle the increase.

He is giving us the wisdom of Joseph in these days. It was the years of waiting and testing that formed the heart of gold and maturity within Joseph to walk out his Kingdom destiny.

Joseph waited thirteen years for his kingship to be established on the throne. There was a deep well of wisdom and maturity that sprang from the Lord, rather than his own abilities. Joseph was stripped of any self-centeredness, self-elevation, and self-indulgence. He became filled with the Spirit of God, with the Spirit of wisdom, during his time in prison.

It was this wisdom that had the maturity of aged wine that flowed out of him to govern and to make sober the intoxicated world. Wisdom brings people and nations into their destiny. Wisdom is the wine of Heaven that sets people free from fleshly foolishness.

LOVE IS JUSTICE

The Lord has not forgotten you. Through it all, He will not forsake the children of His womb. He will not forget the children, born anew of His Spirit!

Can a mother forget the baby at her breast and have no compassion on the child she has borne? Though she may forget, I will not forget you! (Isaiah 49:15)

The Lord loved Joseph and did not forget about him. The Lord loves us and does not leave us stranded in any situation. In His just and perfect love, He is processing out all the junk and gunk from our lives so we can continue to be His righteous ministers of justice. Out of the love and goodness of Joseph's heart, he helped interpret the dreams of both the pharaoh's chief cupbearer and baker. However, as the chief cupbearer was promoted once again, according to the accurate dream interpretation of Joseph, his end of the deal was not fulfilled.

"But when all goes well with you, remember me and show me kindness; mention me to Pharaoh and get me out of this prison. I was forcibly carried off from the land of the Hebrews, and even here I have done nothing to deserve being put in a dungeon." (Genesis 40:14-15)

The chief cupbearer, however, did not remember Joseph; he forgot him. (Genesis 40:23)

The chief cupbearer forgot the agreement he made with Joseph for the next two years! Another two stinking years of being in prison, held on false criminal charges. Another two years of injustice! How much longer would Joseph have to wait? Did God forget? In a time that looked like Joseph's opportunity for deliverance, how could there be such a setback? How could God not come through? Isn't God just?

The Lord wants to place us in positions of influence, governmental authority, and to be the head and not the tail. He has put a voice and a word into our Spirit. He has put Himself inside us. Through it all, the Lord will not and cannot forget about you. This is justice. He is faithful till the end. He will fulfill the word of His mouth. He will fulfill the very things He has promised.

Two years later, when Pharaoh had a disturbing dream, he called for the magicians. Then the cupbearer remembered Joseph and his ability to interpret dreams. Then the Lord brought him up, to the forefront of the stage. This was the moment Joseph had waited thirteen years for!

Did the Lord forget? Did the Lord suddenly remember Joseph and His covenant and promise, or did the Lord always know, in His infinite love and abounding wisdom, exactly the right time to put His plan into action?

And Joseph was thirty years old when he stood before Pharaoh king of Egypt. (Genesis 41:46)

This is justice. This is our God. This is what the Kingdom looks like.

There is a divine time and setting for your favor. There is a divine place and stage for the exaltation of the humble. There is a perfect place for the honoring of the Lord's saints and sons. The Lord is faithful to His people. The Lord is faithful to fulfill all His promises.

All that you are going through and have gone through is for something. It is for a great Kingdom purpose and for the perfect time and place of God's hand to deliver. It isn't just about you, but about giving you a place of Kingdom authority for the salvation of many! Do not lose heart, He is coming back again. Do not lose heart, He is coming back for His people.

God has not forgotten about you and He will not leave you stranded, behind, alone, or defeated. He is Jehovah.

Why, Lord, do you stand far off? Why do you hide yourself in times of trouble? (Psalm 10:1)

The Lord is not slow in keeping his promise, as some understand slowness. Instead he is patient with you, not wanting anyone to perish, but everyone to come to repentance. (2 Peter 3:9)

For the Lord your God is a merciful God; he will not abandon or destroy you or forget the covenant with your ancestors, which he confirmed to them by oath. (Deuteronomy 4:31)

God is the God of Abraham, Isaac, and Jacob who is faithful to the end of the ages. We shall all say of the Lord, "You are our saving justice." YAHWEH, Jehovah Tsidkenu, will be in the mouths of the new breed. Yahweh Our Saving Justice: Look, the days are coming, Yahweh declares, when I shall raise an upright Branch for David; He will reign as king and be wise, doing what is just and upright in the country. In his days Judah will triumph and

Israel will live in safety, and this is the name He will be called
Yahweh-our-saving-justice [Yahweh-tsidkenu] (Jeremiah 23:5-6)

4

THE ROBE OF MANY COLORS

Now Israel loved Joseph more than any of his other sons, because he had been born to him in his old age; and he made an ornate robe for him. (Genesis 37:3)

THE FATHER'S FAVOR

We are people who get to bask in the Father's favor. If you believe it, then you are as favored by God as Joseph was favored by Israel. We are our Father's favorite! We have an ornate robe to wear that is different from the rest of the world.

The Father is thoughtful and careful in all He does. The Bible says Israel favored Joseph and made a robe for him in his old age. Old age can bring impediments to the sight and even distortion and disillusionment to the mind.

Was this robe of many colors an accident? Was it because his father couldn't see properly and accidentally made it in such a way? Were the many colors a mistake, or was it all done on and with purpose? The Lord of all creation does not make mistakes. He is not a God of error. He is not a careless Father, who has slip-ups, goofs, and miscalculations. You are perfect in all your uniqueness. You are perfect in all of your individuality. He has placed His robe of favor and creativity on you for a reason. You are His favorite. It may look odd and different from the rest; it may not fit the standards or fads of the day, but you are His favorite. It may look like an accident or a mess, but you are His masterpiece. You are His perfect artwork, which He gladly boasts in and puts on full display! You are His favorite!

We are in the days of cross-pollination. We are in the days of great unity in midst of diversity. The Lord doesn't want us to conform and try to be like everyone else; He wants us to be ourselves. He wants us to boldly and proudly wear the robe of many colors, the rainbow promises of God's freedom, justice, redemption, and love. The rainbow is a sign of the Lord's love and favor.

The colors we wear are our identity. The uniqueness we each carry is a beautiful name and identity given by the favor of our Heavenly Father.

THE RENAISSANCE MAN

Joseph was a renaissance man. He helped govern all the different streams and rivers that flowed in and out Egypt. He brought forth new life in the darkest of times. The Spirit of wisdom and revelation that lived inside him became a beacon of hope and light, a menorah for all the nations to see and come to.

We are a generation of many colors, many anointings. The Lord is bringing us into a place where our collective robe will be one of many colors. It is no longer just one stream moving, but the convergence of many streams colliding and flowing together as one river. This generation is known as the generation of information. We are so overloaded with so much information that the Lord is giving us wisdom, to become the best.

The many years of Joseph's story were woven into a robe of

many colors. His robe speaks of favor, but also of the many years of learning and becoming.

As a teenager, he was premature in his identity but he still wore the robe of his father's favor. He was young when he received it, but he paid the price to wear it in front of the multitudes years later. God's timing is never late.

All of our stories are like Joseph's robe of many colors. All of our stories are rich with gifts, blessings, trials, and tribulations throughout our journeys. We pick some things up along the way, and later drop them. we drop it. We gain some things and then let them go. We grow and we go. The robes we wear are uniquely designed, like the fingerprint of a person or a snowflake's individuality. There is nothing else like, and there never will be. It is one of a kind. It is an original. And so are you. Don't ever discredit your story or the power of your testimony. Don't ever think that your unique journey is unimportant.

THE RAINBOW CHILDREN

The Lord is restoring and raising His true rainbow children.

Then God blessed Noah and his sons, saying to them, "Be fruitful and increase in number and fill the earth. The fear and dread of you will fall on all the beasts of the earth, and on all the birds in the sky, on every creature that moves along the ground, and on all the fish in the sea; they are given into your hands. Everything that lives and moves about will be food for you. Just as I gave you the green plants, I now give you everything.

"But you must not eat meat that has its lifeblood still in it. And for your lifeblood I will surely demand an accounting. I will demand an accounting from every animal. And from each human being, too, I will demand an accounting for the life of another human being. "Whoever sheds human blood, by humans shall their blood be shed; for in the image of God has God made mankind. As for

you, be fruitful and increase in number; multiply on the earth and increase upon it."

Then God said to Noah and to his sons with him: "I now establish my covenant with you and with your descendants after you and with every living creature that was with you—the birds, the livestock and all the wild animals, all those that came out of the ark with you—every living creature on earth. I establish my covenant with you: Never again will all life be destroyed by the waters of a flood; never again will there be a flood to destroy the earth." And God said, "This is the sign of the covenant I am making between me and you and every living creature with you, a covenant for all generations to come: I have set my rainbow in the clouds, and it will be the sign of the covenant between me and the earth. Whenever I bring clouds over the earth and the rainbow appears in the clouds, I will remember my covenant between me and you and all living creatures of every kind. Never again will the waters become a flood to destroy all life. Whenever the rainbow appears in the clouds, I will see it and remember the everlasting covenant between God and all living creatures of every kind on the earth." So God said to Noah, "This is the sign of the covenant I have established between me and all life on the earth." (Genesis 9:1-17)

The rainbow represents the covenant of God's blessings. The rainbow is a sign in the heavens of God's ultimate faithfulness. The rainbow is a sign of God's prosperity, favor, abundance, and fruitfulness. It is God's covenantal sign of His dominion over all things.

Do not forsake God's colorful sign of His perfect covenant. Do not forsake the sign of His love. Understanding God's heart as displayed in His rainbow is essential to walking out our full destinies here on earth.

I believe Jesus is the grand fulfillment of this rainbow. He is the One who is seated in the clouds, as a sign in the sky and heavenlies. Jesus is our King, our Head, our covering, and is high and above all. He is seated, high and above the waters of the earth, the trials of the world, and the disasters of this fleeting world.

He is seated in peace. He is seated over the waters of the Holy Spirit.

RAINBOW RULE

And He who was sitting was like a jasper stone and a sardius in appearance; and there was a rainbow around the throne, like an emerald in appearance. (Revelation 4:3)

The radiance of God's glory is a rainbow around His throne. All the glorious colors of His nature surround the rule and reign of God. His perfect nature of many colors is a sign of His covenant with Noah and to His people. It is that covenant of peace the Lord sits upon.

We are the rainbow generation crying out for reformation. We are the generation that wants to fully experience the whole expanse of life. We are the generation of many colors. We don't want just one color, but all of them. We don't want to be half-hearted; we zealously desire to be whole-hearted. There is a cry not to be defined or put in a box, but to be free.

The robe of many colors represents the many gifts, strengths, and anointings Joseph received and walked out. However, in the end of his days, Scripture tells us he became governor of Egypt — literally the ruler of the whole known world. All the gifts, anointings, and experiences we've received so far lead us to becoming like King Jesus, who in wisdom knows how to rightly distribute Kingdom blessings all across the earth.

Your story will impact others. Your story will be like bread that will be broken off to feed the multitudes. Your story will be like water that refreshes weary and thirsty souls. I believe our mantles are made up of the best of many mantles. Not only will we have Kathryn Kuhlmans, Billy Grahams, and the multiple mantles of many others, but we will grow into our own mantles. Each is unique and specific to who we are in this time and generation. It is multi-layered and faceted, built up on the foundation of generations. We have the mantle of Jesus Christ Himself. The same Holy Spirit that was inside Jesus is inside us.

The mantle we wear will represent the beauty of the Body of Christ. It displays the beauty of Psalm 133, the unity amongst the brethren. It celebrates the diversity of life and the rich variety of the Kingdom.

Know who you are by remembering where you came from. It is only by understanding that our lives are built upon the foundations of the apostles and prophets (Ephesians 4) that we will properly build upward and move forward. The Lord wants us to be people who don't have to repeat history or reinvent the wheel; our forefathers have become a foundation and a floor from which we are meant to fly forward. Their lives have become a mantle for us to build upon.

We are the generation of the robe of many colors. We are wearing the garment of many colors and materials. We are like the stained-glass windows that richly decorate the rustic church buildings of Europe. Each piece of stained glass has its own unique story, background, history, and beauty. Each window is made up with an array of such rich colors. This is who we are. The new breed is made up with the makeup of many generations, all converging into one.

This convergence is exploding and birthing a new creation—a new breed of lovers, revivalists, reformers, movers and shakers that the world has never seen before! A breed of many colors. A breed of unified and bonafide lovers, who want nothing but the all of God.

THE SCIENCE OF COLOR

Each color manifests a certain type of glory. The majestic colors of the rainbow come from the promises of God, not from the decisions of men. The Lord wants to anoint us to see the beauty in every color. The world is filled with color.

Our eyes are filled with light so the soul can see many colors. The RGB model is the representation and display of images and colors. It is made from three primary colors: red, green, and blue. (RGB). Technology has produced an array of colors through various combinations of these three. The trinity of red, green, and blue is a prophetic display of all the colors coming forth from the Trinity of the Godhead.

With these three primary colors, you can have all the variations that light emits. This three- fold unity of agreement establishes an array of many colors. Don't ever neglect the power of unity. Don't ever neglect the power of agreement.

Without light, there is no color. Without the science of light, there is only color-blindness and blandness. Light manifesting is necessary for the robes of many colors to exist.

A son or daughter of many colors is a son or daughter of light. A child of light is able to emanate not just one color, but many. Reaching the full potential of shining every color is possible when you are a child of light. Don't be limited to manifesting just one. Manifest the whole cornucopia.

Each color releases different sensations, feelings, and vibrations into your spirit, soul, and body. We need a balance and unity of all the different colors, stones and tribes for apostolic and governmental completion.

TWELVE GATES AND FOUNDATIONS OF INTIMACY

One of the seven angels who had the seven bowls full of the seven last plagues came and said to me, "Come, I will show you the bride, the wife of the Lamb." And he carried me away in the Spirit to a mountain great and high, and showed me the Holy City, Jerusalem, coming down out of heaven from God. It shone with the glory of God, and its brilliance was like that of a very precious jewel, like a jasper, clear as crystal.

It had a great, high wall with twelve gates, and with twelve angels at the gates. On the gates were written the names of the twelve tribes of Israel. There were three gates on the east, three on the north, three on the south and three on the west. The wall of the city had twelve foundations, and on them were the names of the twelve apostles of the Lamb.

The angel who talked with me had a measuring rod of gold to measure the city, its gates and its walls. The city was laid out like a square, as long as it was wide. He measured the city with the rod and found it to be 12,000 stadia in length, and as wide and high as it is long. The angel measured the wall using human measurement, and it was 144 cubits thick.

The wall was made of jasper, and the city of pure gold, as pure as glass. The foundations of the city walls were decorated with every kind of precious stone. The first foundation was jasper, the second sapphire, the third agate, the fourth emerald, the fifth onyx, the sixth ruby, the seventh chrysolite, the eighth beryl, the ninth topaz, the tenth turquoise, the eleventh jacinth, and the twelfth amethyst. The twelve gates were twelve pearls, each gate made of a single pearl. The great street of the city was of gold, as pure as transparent glass. (Revelation 21:9-21)

The Lord is building a foundation of His precious stones. The Lord is building a Holy City, Jerusalem, with the beauty of each of the twelve tribes. Each of the twelve walls had a foundation, and on them were the names of the twelve apostles of Jesus. These foundations are apostolic. These foundations are governmental, specific in the character and temperaments of each apostle. The Lord is building these beautiful walls on the names of each apostle.

The foundation of each wall was made of precious stones. Each stone was the stone of each tribe. Each of the twelve tribes of Israel was represented by gemstones on the ephod the high priest would wear when called into the Holy of Holies to minister to the

Lord. They weren't just birthstone, but it destiny stones. Each stone prophetically represented the identity and destiny of each tribe—its unique significance in the Kingdom and in the deep heart of God. None of them were the same, but each was equally important and necessary.

The heart of our Great High Priest, Yeshua, is built up with the beauty of His people, the twelve tribes of Israel. We make up the heart of God. We are the righteousness of Christ. The ephod the high priest wore was a prophetic representation of the strength and solidification of each of the stones of each tribe. The holiness of Jesus beamed and filled each stone on the ephod. It was the Holy City represented on the core, the heart of the Great High Priest, Jesus Christ.

Each of the tribes has a specific gate built upon the foundation. The Apostle John, the writer of the Revelation, states that the Lord is building His gates to be as pure, holy, and beautiful as pearls. Pearls are made from the intensity of deep pressure. Pearls are perfected by the pressures and density of life pressing in.

The Lord is creating a precious pearl out of the door of your heart and the pressures of your life. Don't grow faint or weary. The Lord is creating a pearl out of you.

There are twelve gates and foundations of intimacy. The Lord wants us to be like the stones embedded into the breastplate of the High Priest. We are irreplaceable. Each tribe is uniquely divine and gravely important. The anointing, calling, and strength of each tribe is necessary. The placement of each tribe in the Promised Land is not a coincidence. The allotment of the lands and territories of each tribe is strategically placed with divine order for prosperity.

UNITY

Each tribe is needed in this move of God. It doesn't matter if we're Charismatic, Evangelical, Baptist, or Methodist. Each tribe is needed for the fulfillment of the Gospel. There are gifts and blessings in each person and family that cannot be neglected or ignored. We may not agree with a stream or denomination, but it is by our love for each other that the world will know we are His disciples! It is not by our doctrines or by how well we agree, preach, teach, or have assemblies and meetings. The world will know us by our love. We must learn to celebrate the different gifts and callings of each tribe. Doing this will help strengthen our identity and advance the Kingdom more than we realize.

We cannot neglect or disregard a single part of the Body. We may feel embarrassed by certain members of it, but their existence is necessary for ours. We may feel like the pinky finger is not as important as the heart, but both are absolutely critical in displaying the full manifestation of Christ. Every member of the Body of Christ is crucial in displaying the fullness of Jesus.

The technology of God's Kingdom manifesting in these End Times is going to defy all the laws of physics. The law of love is greater than all natural things.

The Lord is releasing His mantle of the robes of many colors upon this New Breed generation. Be different. Be you. Be the unique, beautiful, rich and diverse blend that you are!

KEEP BEING YOU

So when Joseph came to his brothers, they stripped him of his robe—the ornate robe he was wearing—and they took him and threw him into the cistern. The cistern was empty; there was no water in it. (Genesis 37:23-24)

Don't let anyone take away your robe! Do not let any person or religious spirit take away your unique design in the Lord. The spirit of this age is trying to manipulate and desecrate your beautiful design. Do not let the jealousy of man take away your joy in being the Father's favorite.

People will not always understand you. People will come against you. Your own family, your very flesh and blood, may even throw you under the bus or into the den of lions, but don't let them take away the unique call of God on your life. You may be rejected and you may even be falsely called a heretic. But don't stop being you. As long as it is Biblically sound and lovingly true, be the true you God has created you to be.

Don't be ashamed or apologetic. There is no need to explain. Just be yourself, and the hand of your Father's favor will prosper and promote you. The Father's favor is neither magical nor mystical. It is merciful. It is all because of His mercy that we can be all that we are created to be.

We have been given this incredible favor and inheritance, not because of anything good we've done, but because of the grace of God. The more we grow, the more we come to know our true need for His grace. His grace is enough. It is all because of His grace.

Wearing the robe of many colors of Jesus' righteousness can and will bring out fear, jealousy, hatred, misunderstanding, seclusion, insecurity, and intimidation from men at times. There will be tests, trials, and tribulations—even long waiting periods like Joseph's stint in prison, which lasted 13 years. But rest assured, you are the Father's favorite. The promise will always invite you into a process of maturity, so that you can fully grow up into the mantle.

This new breed is zealously wearing the robe of many colors. This is the righteousness of Christ. This is the sign of His covenant for all generations. We are the new breed.

5

APOSTOLIC GENERATION

We are an apostolic generation, more than we know or understand. The robe of many colors is what we are wearing. We are the generation that wears many different hats and can move in many different giftings and anointings.

We are not limited to one thing or to one stream. We are bursting forth with the many rivers of God's Holy Spirit. There are many gifts inside you. The Holy Spirit is activating His children in these days, so that we can be as He is in this world. (1 John 4:17)

The apostle knows how and when to bring forth a specific gift. He knows the right time to release this person or that thing. He knows when a certain ministry is needed most to bring the corporate to the next level. The apostle is not self-focused, but corporate-focused. From the place of prayer, the apostle moves out to bring the ekklessia forward and closer to fulfilling its Kingdom call and assignment.

The Lord is the God of Abraham, Isaac, and Jacob. He wants us to think generationally. The things of God need to be passed on to the next generation. The true success of any leader is the rate of his succession. How well we transfer the blessings and inheritance of all we've gained and received on to the next generation is what determines our reward. Even while in chains, Paul prayed for open doors!

And pray for us, too, that God may open a door for our message, so that we may proclaim the mystery of Christ, for which I am in chains. (Colossians 4:3)

The Lord is giving us wisdom and prayerful insight to know which doors we are to walk through. The doors He opens cannot be shut by the jurisdiction of man. It is solely the doing of God.

APOSTOLIC KEYS

One of the keys I've learned to use is to stay hungry. One of the ways I stay hungry is to be open to the Lord and to His people. Just because somebody has a bad reputation or negative publicity against them doesn't give me a reason to not listen to them, watch them, or invite them. I want to be wise, but mostly I want to be led by the Lord.

I first choose to be hungry and to listen to the Lord in all things, rather than upholding the word of man. I have learned that a true disciple of Christ can truly learn from any situation and from any person.

A hungry, teachable heart is a key to the apostolic. Being hungry for more of the Lord, to see His Kingdom come, is the purpose of the apostolic. Be hungry. Stay hungry. There is more.

KEY PEOPLE

He who receives you receives Me, and he who receives Me receives the One who sent Me. Whoever receives a prophet because he is a prophet will receive a prophet's reward, and whoever receives a righteous man because he is a righteous man will receive a righteous man's reward. (Matthew 10:40)

There is great blessing when we know whom to receive. There is great blessing when our homes and ministries can become apostolic gateways and portals of the prophetic. God wants to deposit blessings into entire regions through your life. He wants to deposit something that others have received by you receiving them. He wants to deposit the resources of other nations by the routes of trade and exchange. He wants to bring in the spices of India, the silks of Asia, the gold and diamonds of Africa, and the science of Europe through the trade routes. He wants you to be a part of the greatest transference of Kingdom wealth!

Some things can only be received when you go to a certain nation or place in the Spirit. Some things you can only receive when you meet a certain person. There are impartations, treasures, and gems hidden all across the earth. The Lord wants us to be people who can receive and steward all of these Heavenly riches. Be good and God receivers!

HOME OF OBED-EDOM

David was afraid of the Lord that day and said, "How can the ark of the Lord ever come to me?" He was not willing to take the ark of the Lord to be with him in the City of David. Instead, he took it to the house of Obed-Edom the Gittite. The ark of the Lord remained in the house of Obed-Edom the Gittite for three months, and the Lord blessed him and his entire household.

Now King David was told, "The Lord has blessed the household of Obed-Edom and everything he has, because of the ark of God." So David went to bring up the ark of God from the house of Obed-Edom to the City of David with rejoicing. (2 Samuel 6:9-12)

The king of Israel found a simple, normal man He could trust to be the caretaker of this most precious and valuable item—the Ark of God. This man of humility became the caretaker of God's Presence for three months.

What would you have done? Would you have denied this unbelievable opportunity? To some, it would've been a dreadful, fearful thing, but to Obed-Edom, it was a fearful yet joyful matter.

How do we respond when such weighty opportunities are placed before us and decisions need to be made? Would you receive the Ark of God into your home? How would the King of Israel respond to you if you didn't?

Obed-Edom hosted the Ark of the Covenant for a season. Was this a coincidence, or was it for a specific reason that the Ark of God found a temporary home with Obed-Edom's family? I don't think it was a coincidence. Any home and family could've been chosen to house the Ark. However, I believe God chose this home for many reasons. I believe there was a level of preparation and readiness there. It could've been how they kept themselves devoted to the Lord. It could've been that they were a praying family, a God-fearing family. The Bible isn't clear. However, we can imagine why God would've chosen His lot to fall upon the home of Obed- Edom.

The Lord wants to be able to trust us to house His presence—a people who can house glory, His Holy Spirit. The Lord wants us to be ready in and out of season, in the spirit of hospitality, to receive the greatest opportunities that may come suddenly to your door!

Many people cry that they are not blessed enough or don't have this or that. But when they get the very thing they desire, will it change them for worse or for better?

Will you keep your house, heart, and life in order to receive such high-level guests? Are you ready to receive these blessings and mantles?

Our promotion and increase in God's Kingdom often depends on how well we receive a person, a matter, or a test or situation in life. Be a good receiver and by being wise and prayerful in whom and what to receive. It's not your responsibility to receive everybody or all things. However, the Lord will lead you to be apolitically connected to the things of His heart.

ABRAHAM AND THE TRINITY

The Lord appeared to Abraham near the great trees of Mamre while he was sitting at the entrance to his tent in the heat of the day. Abraham looked up and saw three men standing nearby. When he saw them, he hurried from the entrance of his tent to meet them and bowed low to the ground.

He said, "If I have found favor in your eyes, my lord, do not pass your servant by. Let a little water be brought, and then you may all wash your feet and rest under this tree. Let me get you something to eat, so you can be refreshed and then go on your way—now that you have come to your servant." (Genesis 18:1-5)

Abraham recognized that there was something odd about these three men. The Bible says the Lord appeared to Abraham. I don't believe it was just an angel. I believe this was God manifesting Himself in His Trinity form as God the Father, Jesus the Son, and Holy Spirit, all personified. Abraham hurried from his entrance and bowed low to the ground, literally pleading with them to stay with him.

Do we count it an honor to receive a person in our home? Do we count it an honor to serve the poor? Do we count it an honor to only serve those of favor, rather than those who cannot repay you? The Lord wants us to go after our blessings and to make the most of every opportunity.

Abraham washes their feet, helps refresh them, and brings them something to eat. From this encounter, the Lord speaks to Abraham and says, "Right around this time next year, Sarah is going to have a child." The Lord came down and prophesied straight to the hearts of Abraham and Sarah because they received Him into their home.

What would've happened if Abraham approached these three men in a common way? What would've happened if Abraham didn't run after them and bring them into his home? The spirit of hospitality is one of the greatest ways to entertain the angels of God. When you learn to receive the right people into your life, there will be bounteous blessings. There will be prophecy, the Word of the Lord; there will be joy, there will be unity, there will be new life, there will be inheritance.

THE HOME OF LYDIA

From Troas we put out to sea and sailed straight for Samothrace, and the next day we went on to Neapolis. From there we traveled to Philippi, a Roman colony and the leading city of that district of Macedonia. And we stayed there several days.

On the Sabbath we went outside the city gate to the river, where we expected to find a place of prayer. We sat down and began to speak to the women who had gathered there. One of those listening was a woman from the city of Thyatira named Lydia, a dealer in purple cloth. She was a worshiper of God. The Lord opened her heart to respond to Paul's message. When she and the members of her household were baptized, she invited us to her home. "If you consider me a believer in the Lord," she said, "come and stay at my house." And she persuaded us.
(Acts 16:11-15)

Lydia was known as a gatekeeper. A woman became the open door and the apostolic connection to this city. She was a business-woman, an entrepreneur. A woman who dealt purple cloth responded to the message of Paul about this Jesus, King of the Jews. She and her family came to the Lord, thus becoming a major gateway of finances, blessings, connection, and influence. She took in Paul and his friends, and they stayed with her at her home.

This is another example of recognizing who is an apostolic key: People receiving you in their hearts and home is critical. The Lord moves through relationships. Get ready for new and sudden relationships.

When you and I keep our homes, hearts, and even possessions open to the Lord, He will bless us even more. Don't hold back your resources from the Source. Don't be too closed off from the many miraculous ways the Lord may want to bless you and use you.

THE SAMARITAN WOMAN AT THE WELL

Now he had to go through Samaria. So he came to a town in Samaria called Sychar, near the plot of ground Jacob had given to his son Joseph. Jacob's well was there, and Jesus, tired as he was from the journey, sat down by the well. It was about noon.

When a Samaritan woman came to draw water, Jesus said to her, "Will you give me a drink?" (His disciples had gone into the town to buy food.) The Samaritan woman said to him, "You are a Jew and I am a Samaritan woman. How can you ask me for a drink?" (For Jews do not associate with Samaritans.)

Jesus answered her, "If you knew the gift of God and who it is that asks you for a drink, you would have asked him and he would have given you living water." (John 4:4-10)

Do not live your life at such a pace that you miss divine opportunities along the way. Jesus in His humanness stopping to rest at the well quickly became a divine appointment. If Jesus gave Himself an excuse because He was tired, then what an opportunity of harvest He would've missed.

As Jesus stopped to minister refreshment upon the Samaritan woman, she ran back to her village and began testifying about Yeshua. This became open door to bring the whole village to believe the Good News.

You may be tired, but be aware of your surroundings. The Lord may want to do something in the midst of your tiredness. You may be in rest mode, but the Holy Spirit is still searching for His one lost sheep. You may have a million different excuses for shrugging off people and opportunities, but don't miss out on the greatest open doors to the harvest.

Rest assured if you are in His will, you will not miss out on meeting the key, God-sent people that have been appointed to meet you.

DOORWAY OF BLESSINGS

All of these people serve as examples of being doorways of blessings. They became portals the transference of blessings. They played a pivotal role in seeing the Gospel of the Kingdom spread throughout their region.

The Lord wants us to be these types of c connecting points for the Gospel to spread. He wants us to be doors of apostolic connection and blessing. He wants us to have houses where apostolic ministers can stop, rest, deploy, release, and even receive. He wants us to learn to support one another in the advancement of the Kingdom.

Each person has something to give. Each ministry has something to offer. The more we recognize our role in being the apostolic epicenter of connection, the more quickly and strategically the Kingdom will be established in each of our regions.

PAUL AND BARNABAS

Now there were prophets and teachers in Antioch in the church that was there: Barnabas, and Simeon (who was called Niger), and Lucius the Cyrenian, and Manaen (a close friend of Herod the tetrarch), and Saul. And while they were serving the Lord and fasting, the Holy Spirit said, "Set apart now for me Barnabas and Saul for the work to which I have called them." Then, after they had fasted and prayed and placed their hands on them, they sent them away. (Acts 13:1-3)

The Lord commissioned Paul and Barnabas to reach the

Gentiles. There was a strategic partnership in these two men being sent out together.

The Lord said in the beginning it is not good for man to be alone and that He would make a helper suitable for him. (Genesis 2:18)

We are no longer a generation of orphans, lone rangers, and mavericks. The anthem of the heavens is family and unity. The Lord is bringing His people together as the Body of Christ.

The Lord is into key Kingdom partnerships, whether for life-long or seasonal assignments. Whatever the purpose is, we are always interconnected and divinely knitted together.

The Lord will always partner you up with His sons and daughters of encouragement in the fulfillment of His will. Barnabas means "son of encouragement." This name is derived from the Greek word parakletos, which means "one who is summoned to come beside, to help, advocate, and comfort." This is the literal name of the Holy Spirit, the Ruach Qodesh.

The Lord wants us to partner with His Holy Spirit, the Spirit of encouragement, edification, counsel, and exhortation. Yeshua also partnered with the Holy Spirit during His earthly days and ministry. He still does as He is now seated in the heavens.

The Lord wants us to partner with Him in the advancement of the Kingdom, but He also wants us to partner with His key people of encouragement in that process.

You can minister to the hurt, the lost, and the discouraged. However, you cannot partner with the naysayers, the negative Nancys, or those who discourage. You need to partner with those who walk in the Holy Ghost, in the Spirit of encouragement. Be partnered with the Holy Spirit, the parakletos and the people of His Spirit. Not an opposite spirit, but the Spirit of God.

PARTNERSHIPS CREATE PATHWAYS

The Lord is releasing divine partnerships. These strategic partnerships have everything to do what we can give into it, rather than what we can get out of it. These partnerships have everything to do with becoming connecting points for different roads to intersect.

These strategic partnerships have everything to do with being the knots of the nets that are being knitted together. Without the knots, there can be no nets—a which ultimately means there will be no harvest. The Lord is giving us wisdom for strategic partnerships, whether it is for a season or ultimately covenanted for life.

Paul and Barnabas were inseparably partnered for three years to preach the Gospel. History states that Paul and Timothy, his spiritual son, were apostolically connected and aligned for more than a decade. Even while Paul was in prison and going through trials and tribulations, he stood firm as a true father and Timothy stood firm as a true son.

The Lord doesn't want key Kingdom partnerships to divide and be destroyed by arguments and disagreements, as happened with Paul and Barnabas. (Acts 15:3) I believe that type of sharp division between them didn't need to happen. However, the Lord let it happen and turned it around for an even better outcome. Great multiplication and advancement of the Gospel abounded for the glory of Jesus' name.

If you part ways with people, then as much as possible, do so in love and honor. The closeness and proximity of working and walking together may change, but the love we have for one another must not.

Stand firm in giving the right people the right hand of fellowship, not the right-foot of fellowship. Stand firm in wisdom and love. Know who you are to make covenant and to tie knots with. Know how to recognize your strategic partners, to walk and work together to see His harvest and Kingdom come.

Not all people should enter your home. Not all people should know the secrets of your heart. "Don't give the pearls to swine." (Matthew 7:6) There must be mutual trust and safety for these partnerships to work well. And ultimately, it takes love and humility in character.

Time and distance weren't barriers to Paul's love, affection, remembrance, and prayers for those who weren't physically near him. He always kept them in his heart, prayers, and spirit. He always kept them before the Lord, bringing them before the throne of grace in prayer and supplication. This is what we must do as well.

I have not stopped giving thanks for you, remembering you in my prayers. (Ephesians 1:16)

I thank my God every time I remember you. (Philippians 1:3)

PAUL AND TIMOTHY

Prison walls, persecution, false rumors, and accusations against Paul couldn't separate him from Timothy. This partnership was deeper than business. This partnership was family. This partnership was adoption. This partnership was a covenant made between a father and a son.

There are different types of partnerships for different reasons. The Lord is causing us to have wisdom to know who you should be partnered with and open your doors to. The Lord's wisdom is anointing you to see whom you've been destined to closely and intimately become knitted with. Don't be offended if you're not close to somebody at the moment. Give it time. Give them to the Lord. It will happen if it's the Lord's will. All of God's Kingdom purposes will be fulfilled.

There is a time and a season for everything. As long as you stay focused, the Lord will bring you divine contacts and divine appointments. As long as you are committed, the Lord will open doors that no man can open or shut. The hand of the Lord is for those who seek to advance the glory of His name!

Gain wisdom about whom the Lord may be connecting you with and where He may be leading you. It may not make sense, but as long as we are led by the Holy Spirit, it will reap many benefits. It may be sudden, but it can reap a surplus of blessings. It may look and feel unusual, but it may become the new usual.

Get ready for Kingdom partnerships and strategic connections. Begin to open up your hearts and homes, for He's about to pour out His open heavens of blessing and provisions. The Kingdom is advancing through the lives of individuals and families, connecting them in the fellowship of the Holy Spirit.

6

THE ESTHER CALL

When Mordecai learned of all that had been done, he tore his clothes, put on sackcloth and ashes, and went out into the city, wailing loudly and bitterly. But he went only as far as the king's gate, because no one clothed in sackcloth was allowed to enter it. In every province to which the edict and order of the king came, there was great mourning among the Jews, with fasting, weeping and wailing. Many lay in sackcloth and ashes. When Esther's eunuchs and female attendants came and told her about Mordecai, she was in great distress. She sent clothes for him to put on instead of his sackcloth, but he would not accept them. Then Esther summoned Hathak, one of the king's eunuchs assigned to attend her, and ordered him to find out what was troubling Mordecai and why. (Esther 4:1-5)

Then she instructed him to say to Mordecai, "All the king's officials and the people of the royal provinces know that for any man or woman who approaches the king in the inner court without being summoned the king has but one law: that they be put to death unless the king extends the gold scepter to them and spares their lives. But thirty days have passed since I was called to go to the king." When Esther's words were reported to Mordecai, he sent back this answer: "Do not think that because you are in the king's house you alone of all the Jews will escape. For if you remain silent at this time, relief and deliverance for the Jews will arise from another place, but you and your father's family will perish. And who knows but that you have come to your royal position for such a time as this?" (Esther 4:10-14)

SUCH A TIME AS THIS

Recognize your time; recognize your hour. Recognize the signs of the times you are living in. You were born for such a time as this! There is no other day like the one we are living in now. Now is the time for you to step out and to walk into your call and destiny. You can't be silent anymore. Too many people have kept their mouths closed for fear of persecution. Too many Christians have been wimps, acting like they have no backbone. However, the Lord is about to roar out of them, like a lion roaring at injustice. The spirit of righteousness cannot and will not stay silent anymore. We do not want blood on our hands, but that's what we'll get if we don't speak up now with the truth.

The veils on peoples' faces, the bits in peoples' mouths, the false coverings and spirits of fear and religion are all coming off! Every unholy thing that has held you back will no longer strangle you! It is time to put every hindering thing aside and far away from us.

The Spirit of Christ's righteousness is rising up out of the mouths of people in this hour, especially women. The Lord is anointing women to rise up with a voice and a Word from Heaven. These women (and men) will rise up for life.

The Pharisees and Sadducees came to Jesus and tested him by asking him to show them a sign from heaven. He replied, "When evening comes, you say, 'It will be fair weather, for the sky is red,' and in the morning, 'Today it will be stormy, for the sky is red and

overcast.' You know how to interpret the appearance of the sky, but you cannot interpret the signs of the times. A wicked and adulterous generation looks for a sign, but none will be given it except the sign of Jonah." Jesus then left them and went away.
(Matthew 16:1-4)

The Lord wants us to interpret the signs. The times are ripe and ready for a flooding and an outpouring of the Holy Spirit.

KINGDOM PROTOCOL

There is a certain order for things that need to be done. There was an order to how the Lord created everything as written in Genesis. The stars and the planets hold the solar system together. The water holds the lands together. The land is the platform for the creatures to inhabit. thus allowing human beings to come to life. There is an order to all things.

God is a God of order. Heaven can sometimes look contrary and even crazy compared to what is seen in this realm. However, the ways of the Kingdom are much higher and greater than our human, finite minds have created, and the Lord wants us to be as high as He is. Our carnal minds limit us. When we allow the Word to renew and rejuvenate our minds, we come up into His mind and think upon the things that are above.

Before receiving the Lord and the Holy Spirit, one must confess and repent from sins. There is a purpose and an order in this. In order to gain the more of God, there are certain steps of engagement that need to be completed.

In order to gain a harvest, one must choose the ground that is good for sowing, then till and plow the land. After that, seeds are sown. Then they must be watered regularly as they grow, weeding throughout the process to keep the plants healthy. Eventually there will be a harvest! And then one must thresh the wheat from the chaff.

One must begin to separate what is good and bad. What must

begin to discern what is of the Lord and not. There is great work to be done. It all starts with understanding the God of order.

The God of the heavenly courts wants you to triumphantly come into the Presence of the Living God in the holy of holies. Enter in with thanksgiving and praise. Enter in with extravagant dance and praise like David did in bringing in the Ark of God.

There are countless Biblical examples and stories that mirror this great Kingdom principle. Allow the Lord to lead you into Kingdom protocol for the greatest breakthroughs of your life.

JESUS IS THE GOLDEN PROTOCOL

When he saw Queen Esther standing in the court, he was pleased with her and held out to her the gold scepter that was in his hand. So Esther approached and touched the tip of the scepter."
(Esther 5:2)

Then the king extended the gold scepter to Esther and she arose and stood before him." (Esther 8:4)

In Christ Jesus, the golden scepter is graciously stretched out toward you because of what the Lord has done! Because of His great and merciful sacrifice, you can boldly come before the throne of grace and carry out your call. Because of the smearing of the blood and the tearing of the body, you can victoriously walk out in the power of the Lord.

Jesus is the protocol! Being led by the Spirit of love is the protocol! The blood of the Lamb is the protocol! Understanding the finished work of Jesus and maturing into that reality is the protocol! Jesus is enough!

Lean into the substance and the true Kingdom norm. Don't just try to fulfill the many steps and countless statutes of the Law, but receive the grace of the Holy Spirit, for Jesus has fulfilled the Law!

The scepter was a sign of the king's judgment. It was the sign for death or for life. The king extending his golden scepter was a matter of fear and great respect.

Now in Christ Jesus, you have the favor! You have been called and appointed in the sight of the king. He has stretched his golden scepter toward you.

OUT OF ORDER

This is amazing grace should not be neglected. It must be respected, because it is by grace that we are saved and have been called and commissioned. It is by grace that we can all enter in. Not just the elites, the well educated, or the children of privilege; we all can graciously enter in before the Lord.

He has called us all to be part of the royal priesthood. We can all prophesy. We can all lay our hands on the sick and heal them. We can all dream big dreams! The Kingdom of our God is big! Think big! Dream big! Get involved and go out and live life to the full in Jesus' name! Your small thinking and boxed-in dreaming does nobody any good. Your overly careful living, controlled plans and comfortable schedules do not bring great glory to the King.

Being in Christ in intimacy and love is the Heavenly protocol. When we are in Christ and are led by His Holy Spirit, there is no failure. There is no getting struck to death like Uzzah when he naively stretched out his hand and touched the Ark of God while trying to save it from tipping over. Being out of order means being out of the Spirit. Those who are led by the Spirit are in Heavenly order. Let the Spirit order and direct your steps. There is only victory and righteous living with the perfect leading of the Holy Spirit.

The Lord has stretched out His golden scepter and is calling you up and out, higher. He has called you by name to go where He is! No more delay and no more disobedience. It is time for utmost obedience and surrender to His glorious will, to partner with the royal, holy will of the Father. He has written it. He has done it.

THE HIDDEN HADASSAHS

The Lord is raising up Hadassahs all across the earth.

Mordecai had a cousin named Hadassah, whom he had brought up because she had neither father nor mother. This young woman, who was also known as Esther, had a lovely figure and was beautiful. Mordecai had taken her as his own daughter when her father and mother died. (Esther 2:7)

Hadassah is Esther's original name, before she was given the Persian name by which which is best known. "Esther" was an outward identity for a Jewish woman inwardly named Hadassah. The true Hadassah couldn't be ignored or hide forever. Her true nature eventually needed to come out. You truth will always come out. There is no hiding when the light within you shines aloud.

There are many things the Lord has instilled within us, and He is bringing all such things to birth. The baby must come out! Too many of us have been pregnant for too long. The three trimesters are up and the clock is done ticking. It's time for the world to see the crown of the baby and it's time for the world to hear the babes' cry! Cry out loud world! Cry out loud!

Hadassah also is a type myrtle tree found in Israel. Hadassahs have dark green leaves all around. The flowers are beautiful and fragrant—pure white with purple rims. These Hadassah flowers are filled with purity and outlined with royalty. This is holy unto the Lord.

This is like the women God is raising up now. The world may be in darkness, but these beautiful flowers will bloom and blossom, releasing the most pleasant of fragrances not only in Israel but across the earth! Amid the dark leaves, the Hadassah flowers will bloom and boldly shine their vibrant purity, prudence, and holiness.

In the darkest of times, the purity of God will shine in the hearts of men and women. These people will be wrapped in glory and royalty. The glory of God is the royalty of pure hearts.

The pure in heart will bloom and blossom Kingdom favor. This is the Lord's doing. The power of purity is the royalty of women. The power of purity is the favor of the Lord. The power of purity is what will change a nation. These Hadassahs are beautifully ornamenting the earth.

HADASSAHS OF PURITY

There is great power in women. The Lord is raising up women to be victorious Proverbs 31 women. The Esther call is not just for women; it is for both genders, men and women. However, there is a specific focus on women now.

There are some things only women can do, and some they honestly do best. There's something about His daughters that can move the heart of Papa God. Anointed women of God can turn the hearts of men like no one else—even the hearts of dictators, rulers, governors and people of influence. Women are powerful, and the Lord is raising up those who know their identity. God is raising up Esthers, Hadassahs, who are not afraid to stand up against the evils of society; women who are not afraid of the trickery, vices, and deceptions of the devil. Women who rise up in obedience as the brave and chosen Bride of Christ!

WISDOM AND BEAUTY IN THE HIDDEN PLACE

Then Esther sent this reply to Mordecai: "Go, gather together all the Jews who are in Susa, and fast for me. Do not eat or drink for three days, night or day. I and my attendants will fast as you do. When this is done, I will go to the king, even though it is against the law. And if I perish, I perish." So Mordecai went away and carried out all of Esther's instructions. (Esther 4:16-17)

Esther didn't shy away from this opportunity. She knew the

Lord's lot had fallen into her lap. She turned to the Lord in prayer and cried out for deliverance. Only God could save the desperate band of Israelites.

Esther knew how to use the power of unified prayer and fasting. Esther knew what to do because she humbled herself in prayer. She cried out to God, and the Lord deposited great wisdom into her spirit. How she turned the heart of the king could only be explained by the hand of God.

She threw a banquet in the king's honor. Her beauty was irresistible. The Lord is raising up people who are so saturated in the heavy presence of God that there will be an undeniably different spirit and aroma about us.

On the third day Esther put on her royal robes and stood in the inner court of the palace, in front of the king's hall. The king was sitting on his royal throne in the hall, facing the entrance. When he saw Queen Esther standing in the court, he was pleased with her and held out to her the gold scepter that was in his hand. So Esther approached and touched the tip of the scepter.

Then the king asked, "What is it, Queen Esther? What is your request? Even up to half the kingdom, it will be given you." "If it pleases the king," replied Esther, "let the king, together with Haman, come today to a banquet I have prepared for him." "Bring Haman at once," the king said, "so that we may do what Esther asks." So the king and Haman went to the banquet Esther had prepared. As they were drinking wine, the king again asked Esther, "Now what is your petition? It will be given you. And what is your request? Even up to half the kingdom, it will be granted."

Esther replied, "My petition and my request is this: If the king regards me with favor and if it pleases the king to grant my petition and fulfill my request, let the king and Haman come tomorrow to the banquet I will prepare for them. Then I will answer the king's question." (Esther 5:1-8)

With utmost wisdom and beauty, Esther won the heart and favor of the king. The glory she embodied couldn't be rejected. With the Spirit of wisdom on her side, Esther couldn't be denied.

The king offered her up to half of the kingdom! She purposefully built up anticipation so her request on the second day would surely be set in motion. She had been anointed to gain justice for the people of God. Her request would be answered!

You please the king. You please the Father. You bring pleasure to the God of love. You were made for love. You were made for pleasure. You were made to have great favor in His eyes.

It is the grace of God, the new wine of the Holy Spirit, that will win hearts. It is the love banquet of Jesus that will bring in the harvest. It is the feasts and festivals, the celebrations of God, that release prophetic power and deliverance.

Esther was the life of the party. She was dipped in aloes, myrrhs, oils, and perfumes for months before meeting the king. She was being trained to be the best of the best. And she was deeply immersed and saturated in the Holy Spirit. She became one with the Anointed One, with the very oil of Heaven.

God is anointing people in the hidden place to courageously slay the Goliaths of our day with what looks like great ease and unbelievable skill. What would've taken a year is being done in a day. What would usually take a decade will take a week.

If we choose to submit to His process, then our bill will be processed. If we simply choose to be His adopted children, then we will gain great inheritance that is only obtained through miraculous intervention.

God will use every single detail of our lives to bring us to sudden moments for such a time as this. Esther's humble hiddenness in the Lord, being prepared in the secret place, was the secret to her promotion. Even before this preparation, she was being trained by her uncle Mordecai in the ways of the Lord.

All of our hidden times with the Lord are for a purpose. Don't lose heart, your promotion is near. Don't grow faint. Your promotion is right around the corner. Do not forsake the hidden place. Do not move rashly out of your times of training.

All this training prepared Esther to walk out great Kingdom transformation with humble wisdom. She received insight that brought forth great justice for the Jews, the people of God. She gained such favor with the king that her plea was undeniable, and it was granted with swift authority.

We are favored in the Lord's sight. We stand out from and above the rest. We are not average humans; we are children of God. We are not average Joes, we are abnormal Heavenly beings who are not of this world. Do not be fooled by appearances; wait for the manifestation of Christ.

CHOOSING THE LEAST LIKELY

Now Lot, who was moving about with Abram, also had flocks and herds and tents. But the land could not support them while they stayed together, for their possessions were so great that they were not able to stay together. And quarreling arose between Abram's herders and Lot's. The Canaanites and Perizzites were also living in the land at that time.

So Abram said to Lot, "Let's not have any quarreling between you and me, or between your herders and mine, for we are close relatives. Is not the whole land before you? Let's part company. If you go to the left, I'll go to the right; if you go to the right, I'll go to the left."

Lot looked around and saw that the whole plain of the Jordan toward Zoar was well watered, like the garden of the Lord, like the land of Egypt. (This was before the Lord destroyed Sodom and Gomorrah.) So Lot chose for himself the whole plain of the Jordan and set out toward the east. The two men parted company: Abram lived in the land of Canaan, while Lot lived among the cities of the plain and pitched his tents near Sodom.

Now the people of Sodom were wicked and were sinning greatly against the Lord. (Genesis 13:5-13)

Abram chooses the land that looks least likely to bear great fruit. Isn't this much like God? The Lord tends to choose to least likely things to be miraculous signs and wonders.

Abram allows his nephew Lot to choose the better land. However, it was positioned near Sodom and Gomorrah, which was the ultimate land of sin. I believe the land Lot chose was produced by the false powers of the gods of the Canaanites. Lot did not have eyes to see or ears to hear, so he therefore was led foolishly by the understanding of his carnal nature. Don't judge a book by its cover. Don't just do church by a schedule. Come up higher and be led by the Holy Spirit.

Abraham chose the land that was less pleasing. However, this was the land that began to bear a great harvest. Allow the Lord to bear fruit in the areas of barrenness because of your obedience to abide in the Vine of Grace. Where there is grace, the branches will bear great plenty.

God is in the business of choosing the least likely people and turning them into giants. The Lord is in the business of transforming dry and desolate lands into flourishing cities, teeming with life. God is revolutionizing the earth! He wants us to not despise the days of small beginnings but to allow His grace to prosper all that we are and do.

THE NAMELESS AND FACELESS

Hadassah may have been an orphan girl, adopted by her older cousin Mordecai, but she shined as the valiant and wise Queen Esther. She turned the heart of God and the heart of the king to save the Jewish people. Great justice was released and history made.

God is raising up the nameless and faceless—regular, average, normal people, to take the lead. These "average Joes" will change the world. This new breed will not be concerned about or focused on fame. They will have a deep conviction for purity and God's presence; for character and anointing; for the harvest of souls and the jubilee of God's people.

God is raising up the hidden Hadassahs, the little shepherd Davids, the loud and angry fishermen like Peter. God is raising up the new breed.

Don't let your past hold you back. God loves to use the weak to humble the strong. Don't let your shame or your inadequacies and insecurities hold you back. You were born to be used by God for such a time as this.

There is a royal commissioning by the love of God. You have found favor in His eyes. The Lord has been waiting for you to rise and shine and to take your place. Only you can do what you have been called to do.

7

ROYAL COMMISSIONING

There is a royal commissioning taking place. The Lord is calling
out His people.

Then the king extended the gold scepter to Esther and she arose
and stood before him." (Esther 8:4)

How much longer must this golden scepter be stretched
out? How much longer must the Lord of Hosts wait for
an answer? Who will answer His call? Who will go?

SONS BEING REVEALED

For the creation waits in eager expectation for the children of
God to be revealed. (Romans 8:19)

This word, revealed, is apokálypsis, which means "properly
uncovering." It is also the last book of the Bible; Revelation or the
Apocalypse.

This word is also defined as "a laying bare, making naked." The
Lord is making bare His great Son, Who has been hidden in His

earthly sons and daughters. He is making bare His great treasures in the maps of the world. He is unveiling and uncovering the ones who have been prepared and made ready for such a time as this.

There are more of the new breed than you know. This new breed has been steeping in the depths of the Spirit, getting ready for a revolution. The sons are about to be revealed. We are in the times of the great Apocalypse!

The word apostle, which means, "sent out ones," comes from the same root word as apocalypse. The apostle of the five-fold ministry, the apostolic office, is the apocalypse, the revealing, the revelation of Christ Jesus.

We often think we're waiting on God, when in reality, God is waiting on us. All of creation has been moaning and groaning, waiting for the full-blown life of the sons of God to manifest. God wants your promotion more than you do! God is the One who is love and is long-suffering. But He can't hold Himself back any longer. He is itching to show His glory through you and me. This is the Gospel. This is our Father. He wants to put His Son, Jesus, on display through the beautiful example of our daily lives. He wants to show off the beauty and the perfection of His Son in and through us.

God is zealously jealous to see His will done in our lives. He is more committed to us than we are to Him. His "I do" is forever. He has committed to be in and with us for all eternity. He has moved in, with all of His glory and splendor, and He is not moving out. He has found the perfect home inside of you and me. He is satisfied with temple He has fashioned for Himself in our hearts. You and I are fit for the dwelling of a King—and not just any king, but the King of kings.

THE ROYAL POTTER

Yet you, LORD, are our Father. We are the clay, you are the potter; we are all the work of your hand. (Isaiah 64:8)

History tells us that Joseph, Jesus' adopted father, was a carpenter (Matthew 13:55). In fact, Greek word for "carpenter" is teckton, which means "builder." Most likely, Jesus' father was a builder of stone and rocks.

In the Jewish culture, Jesus would take up his father's trade and inherit this role in the community. It is commonly understood that Jesus was a carpenter of wood before being called into the carpentry of men.

Our Heavenly Father is the great potter. He has placed His very hands upon us and sent us out. We have the signature of the Holy Spirit written on our lives. We are wearing His signet ring. As He carved the Law of Moses into the rock tablets by His finger, He has written the law of love on our hearts.

Then the LORD God formed a man from the dust of the ground and breathed into his nostrils the breath of life, and the man became a living being. (Genesis 2:7)

Genesis 1-3 tells us He created almost everything by speaking it into being—but He created man and woman with His own hands. He made Adam out of clay, as an earthen vessel.

Moses, the original author and writer of Genesis, did not write this metaphorically. He wrote it with detail for a reason: To display God's heart in using His hands to create us, His children.

As a surgeon carefully pulls the newborn baby from the mother's body, Jesus pulls us out of the dust of the earth with His miraculous hands. We are His handiwork. We are His perfect workmanship; His masterpiece.

We are made in the image and the glory of God. He is the Potter and we are the clay. We are all the work of His hands.

INTIMACY TO DESTINY

God is more excited and passionate about fulfilling the Great Commission than we are. He is more emotionally moved to seeing souls saved and the Kingdom advanced than our Western Christian religion has led us to believe. God is happy, He is joyful, and He is hopefully waiting for many sons come to Him!

He wouldn't place His anointing inside us if He didn't want us to use it. It is essential for you to step up and out into the high and heavenly will of God. The earth has been waiting. He didn't save you just so you can be a good Christian. He saved you and raised you so you can save and raise others.

He is not stingy with His grace, nor is He cheap with His mercy. He is gracious, generous, and wise in His investments. You are His greatest investment. You are His greatest resource in Christ Jesus. In all of God's infinite wisdom, He has chosen you and me to be one-of-a-kind children, to walk out something so dynamic and huge that we can only do. It is not the same without you playing your part.

Jesus can't help but send out His people. The nation of Israel became too comfortable and fat in their blessings and forgot the reason for their existence, which was to be a light for the nations. So Jesus took that mandate and gave it to us Gentiles, so that we can each bear the light of the Gospel and bring illumination to all nations.

God is establishing His Kingdom, His government, here on this earth. He is releasing His nature and DNA so the earth will be a reflection of Heaven.

The Lord is the head apostle of our faith. He wants the Bride of Christ to not only enjoy her salvation, but to be a shining light for the nations. He wants the Bride not only to enjoy Him in intimacy in the King's chambers, but to rule and reign the whole Kingdom. It is ours, so don't be stuck in the chambers. The whole land is under our dominion; don't get caught slumbering in one room. The Kingdom is the land of plenty and abundance. God is a big God.

ESTABLISHED BY TWO OR THREE

He wants to send us out, even by two by two. There is power in agreement. There is power in unity. Jesus said, "Where two or three are gathered, I am there" (Matthew 18:20). The validity of our testimony is established by two or three witnesses. This also is how the government of Heaven is established. Therefore God Himself is known as the Trinity. That is why there were seven pairs of every clean animal that entered the ark of Noah, along with one pair of every unclean animal. There was a partnership of male and female of each creature for the purpose of reproduction.

God wants to reproduce His government through us. Partnerships, teamwork, and unity are necessary for a greater birthing of His Kingdom.

JESUS SENDS OUT THE 72

After this the Lord appointed seventy-two others and sent them two by two ahead of him to every town and place where he was about to go. He told them, "The harvest is plentiful, but the workers are few. Ask the Lord of the harvest, therefore, to send out workers into his harvest field. Go! I am sending you out like lambs among wolves. Do not take a purse or bag or sandals; and do not greet anyone on the road.

"When you enter a house, first say, 'Peace to this house.' If someone who promotes peace is there, your peace will rest on them; if not, it will return to you. Stay there, eating and drinking whatever they give you, for the worker deserves his wages. Do not move around from house to house. "When you enter a town and are welcomed, eat what is offered to you. Heal the sick who are there and tell them, 'The kingdom of God has come near to you.' But when you enter a town and are not welcomed, go into its streets and say, 'Even the dust of your town we wipe from our feet as a warning to you. Yet be sure of this: The kingdom of God

has come near.' I tell you, it will be more bearable on that day for Sodom than for that town. (Luke 10:1-11 NIV)

There is a royal commissioning by the hands and authority of Jesus. He has commanded us to enter neighborhoods, towns, cities, and countries in His name. We are to proclaim the Gospel. We are to heal the sick and tell them the Kingdom is near!

The proclamation and demonstration of the Kingdom is all about His peace. That is why Jesus says, "When you enter a house, first say, 'Peace to this house.' " The Gospel of the Kingdom is all about the peace of Jesus!

Truly the harvest is plentiful. The Lord is commissioning us to go, to sow and to reap. To be a part of the greatest harvest of souls and spoils that we have yet to see.

Jesus said, "Go!" He is sending us! Go! Go into the harvest fields of the world! Go into the seven mountains of society! Go, go, go! The heart of the Lord is to transform His people from being mere pew-sitters to people who walk out their faith in power and in Spirit.

We are living in an apostolic age, when it's no longer about gatherings and meetings, but going out of the church walls and doing the Kingdom stuff.

People are sick and tired of the talk; people are aching for the real deal, the authentic walk. Not for people who act like they have it all and know it all, but people who walk in humility and vulnerability before the world. Go, go, go!

HIS BREATH COMMISSIONS

Again Jesus said, "Peace be with you! As the Father has sent me, I am sending you." And with that he breathed on them and said, "Receive the Holy Spirit. If you forgive anyone's sins, their sins are forgiven; if you do not forgive them, they are not forgiven." (John 20:21-23)

Jesus sent His fearful disciples out by breathing the life of Heaven upon them. The atmosphere of Heaven is the peace of Jesus. This peace commissioned them and settled power and grace in their hearts to walk out their mighty call in Christ.

Jesus blows His breath upon His disciples, and they receive the Holy Spirit. This was the foretaste of receiving the Holy Spirit at Pentecost, which eventually led them to being baptized in fire. God is blowing His fresh breath across the earth, upon ordinary people like you and me, made from the dust of the earth. It is His breath that causes us to do the supernatural. It is His breath that allows us to do the miraculous. He has blown His Holy Spirit into us, so that we may no longer be a valley of dry bones, but a thriving, powerful Body of Christ.

His breath commissions us to be good, not bad; to have good breath, not bad breath! To be the fragrance of love, not the stink of rotting flesh.

God has commissioned us to co-create with Him, on this earth, His Kingdom realm. He wants us to be not mere people of the dust and earth, but His people of heavenly Kingdom substance.

If He wanted us to be regular, average people, He would've left us as mere dust. The earthly elements are fine, but they're not the same substance as God. It is His breath within us that causes us to do His mighty Kingdom works and enables us to walk as Him. Without the miraculous breath of God, we would be as mundane as the rest of creation. However, the Lord has anointed us not just as created beings but to be creating beings.

BREATH OF CHANGE

We have God's breath so we can bring a dying world back to life. We have the breath of the Holy Spirit, this intimate communion, so we can rule and reign. We have the very life source of Heaven within us so He can flow and blow through us. We are conduits of Heaven's conduct. We are ambassadors of God's Kingdom.

The breath of God is the wind of change. The Lord is commissioning change through the fresh breath of the Holy Spirit. There is change coming because there is forgiveness! Where the Holy Spirit is, there is forgiveness. This lies at the foundation of peace.

Our Lord Jesus is commissioning us by blowing and breathing His Holy Spirit upon and into us, as He did with Adam. Except now, the Holy Spirit is poured out at an even greater measure.

It brings the Lord glory for us to go out in His name, not to stay the same in our own ways. The Holy Spirit never leaves us as we are. His love changes us to be more and more like Him, which is how we become our true selves.

There is a royal commissioning happening across the earth. The Lord is sending forth His people, stretching out His golden scepter, for such a time as this. You have gained the favor of the Lord, so therefore, you can go out in His name.

DISCERNING YOUR TIME

On the third day a wedding took place at Cana in Galilee. Jesus' mother was there, and Jesus and his disciples had also been invited to the wedding. When the wine was gone, Jesus' mother said to him, "They have no more wine." "Woman, why do you involve me?" Jesus replied. "My hour has not yet come." His mother said to the servants, "Do whatever he tells you."
(John 2:1-5)

God is anointing His people to understand the urgency of the hour and the mandate of Heaven. Jesus is giving His people a spirit of discernment to understand the signs and the times, to recognize the hour of people.

When we understand the time we have stepped into, the vortex of suddenlies will overtake us. Suddenly moments are ordered and aligned into the steps of those who discern their times.

THE TIME IS NOW

Was it possible that Mary, the mother of Jesus, understood or saw something in Him that He didn't? Jesus said it wasn't His time; however, Mary, totally ignoring what He said, continued to push Jesus to the center of the platform. It was time for Jesus to work a miracle.

The Bible says the miracle of changing water into wine at the wedding in Cana revealed His glory. Was it too soon? Is there a purpose in all of this?

Is our too soon actually too soon? Are all of our excuses of not feeling ready actually right, or are they meaningless? Are we making more excuses than disciples? When is the time really right?

There really is no perfect timing. As I've talked with many people about getting married or having children, I've asked, "Are you ready?" Most of them say they don't know if they'll ever be ready—but they are!

Stop waiting for your perfect sign to fall from the sky. Stop waiting for your list of prayers to be answered before you praise Him. Stop waiting for God to be a vending machine and making it all about how you want it and when you want it. Christianity is not Burger King. You can't have it your way. Get in His way and live a life of trust and surrender. He's been waiting for you!

Too many people wait for another impartation or another person to lay their hands on them in prayer. Too many people are waiting to be sent out by their pastor while sadly sitting and doing nothing. Religion has made it impossible to see people promoted and celebrated, singling out certain personalities to take the center stage, rather than activating a whole Body to do the work. It is essential for people to be hidden and trained, to sit under and serve a man or woman of God for an amount of time until showing themselves approved. However, too many churches have put too many rules and regulations on people, making it hard for them to become the head.

Don't come under leadership that is more concerned with

church programs and building funds (as genuinely important as those things are). Come under the anointing of a leader who is more interested in empowering people to fulfill the callings and mandates on their lives. After all, every one of us is accountable to God to what we do in His name.

That is why it's essential to have people and opportunities around us that bring out the best in us. Christianity is not about being stowed away, alone and isolated in a prayer closet; it is being out and about with people, making yourself available to all who may come. Mary recognized that the wedding was an invitation for Jesus' greater glory to be shown.

Jesus loves weddings; the covenant of the new wine of the Holy Spirit is manifested in the marriage supper of the Lamb.

When you are in love with Jesus, every time is the right time, to reveal His glory! Wherever you go, wherever you are, reveal the glory of God's perfect love.

Make the most of every opportunity, no matter how small or how big it may seem. Be like Jesus. The Lord wants us to make the most of every opportunity that is brought before us. This is why we must be ready in and out of season. When we are prepared for whatever comes, we will respond as Jesus would.

Doing the little things along the way gets us prepared for the big opportunities. Saying yes and amen in the secret place, when no one is looking, gets our hearts in the right posture for when the blessings, promotions, and crowds come. Do you understand the time that is at hand?

Too many people have been held back. The Lord of the Harvest is placing people into their proper positions, to be launched out as sickles in the harvest. The winds of the Holy Spirit are blowing among the workers and worshippers. The winds of the Holy Spirit are setting the captives free so to make captivity itself captive. The Holy Spirit is hand-choosing His few to will rise up as the true ekklessia they are meant to be.

There are too many people hurting. It is not time for us to play church anymore. The time for people to quietly sit or stand on command among the pews once or twice a week is no longer good enough. People are hungry for the more. People want to see the God of the Scriptures.

DO NOT MISS HIS VISITATION

Too many people have been in a wrong church wineskin. They have been trained in an old, traditional mindset, which has produced, fat, lazy, comfortable Christians. Jesus is commissioning and pushing us out from our chairs and into the harvest field. The Lord is calling us by name, moving us into the place of being chosen and not just called.

When Jesus rode into Jerusalem on a donkey, He wept, because He said the city missed the hour of His visitation (Luke 19:41). Are we so busy searching the Scriptures that we miss the Living Word? Are we so busy with our programs and church schedules that we miss the Holy Spirit in our services? Are we so busy with our own agendas that we miss what the Lord wants to do in that very moment?

You study the Scriptures diligently because you think that in them you have eternal life. These are the very Scriptures that testify about me, yet you refuse to come to me to have life.
(John 5:39 NIV)

Let's not get so busy being Christians that we forget about Jesus. Let's not get so caught up with playing church that we forsake first love. Jesus is here. Jesus is here.

Let God interrupt your plans. Let God interrupt what you think is right and good. Let God destroy your self-centered sense of entitlement and control, and let Him lead you into glories unknown. Let God be both mysterious and revealing to you today.

Do not miss the hour of God's visitation. Do not miss out on the more of what God has for you. The new breed is not satisfied with the mediocre, but craves the miraculous. The new breed is not comfortable with mere head knowledge, but is starving for action and application. The new breed is not settling for dead religion, but are churning with an appetite to see Heaven invading earth.

A true leader is not insecure around powerful people. A true leader wants their people to be powerful. A true leader makes room for others to be freely and wisely powerful in the Lord. They are not insecure, jealous, or fearful of what may be. They fear the Lord and therefore trust in the Lord's anointing more than they give way to the enemy.

THE GREAT COMMISSION

Then the eleven disciples went to Galilee, to the mountain where Jesus had told them to go. When they saw him, they worshiped him; but some doubted. Then Jesus came to them and said, "All authority in heaven and on earth has been given to me. Therefore go and make disciples of all nations, baptizing them in the name of the Father and of the Son and of the Holy Spirit, and teaching them to obey everything I have commanded you. And surely I am with you always, to the very end of the age."
(Matthew 28:16-20)

Even after Jesus' resurrection, some doubted. How much longer are we going to doubt Jesus? Do not let doubt and unbelief rob you of your royal commissioning. We are the new breed.

Jesus has commissioned us to stomp out Hell. He has commissioned us to take back what the enemy has stolen, in His resurrected nature and finished work, and to bring forth restoration and restitution all across the earth. All of creation is in bondage, waiting for us, the sons of God, to set it free into the fullness of Christ.

Jesus regained the deed to the earth, which Adam and Eve gave up to the devil. The deed was sneakily stolen away like the cheap birthright that was traded in for a bowl of soup. The devil is and always will be the father of lies, who steals, kills, and destroys. He is the lord of deception.

Jesus, on the cross at Mount Golgotha, regained the deed to the earth realm by dying as an innocent man, the unblemished Lamb of God. He fulfilled every righteous requirement that was in the Law and He died as us. He became sin, who knew no sin, so that we might become His righteousness. Then in His resurrection, He rose again as us, so that in Him, we could rule and reign all across the earth once again, as God originally intended.

Jesus regained the deed to the earth and He gave it to us, His holy children, once again! He has given us not only power but His authority to fully take dominion and inhabit the earth as God does in Heaven.

By that right of entitlement and that Kingdom authority, He commands us to go! Go and make disciples! Turn every stubborn goat nation into a sheep nation that follows and heeds the word of their Shepherd. Go, go, go, go, go!

Go and live your dream! Go and write your book! Go and start your business! Go and get right with your family! Go and travel the world! Go and start your family! No more delays and no more hindrances!

Jesus has commissioned and commanded you to be like Him and to take dominion of all things. This is not a choice. This is not an option. Go.

The Lord wants to send us out to the peoples of all nations. The new breed will joyfully go out into the mission fields of the world. The new breed will be eager to sacrifice and spend themselves for the sake of the Gospel. They will go out into the four corners of the earth to make the Gospel known.

The new breed will willingly lay their lives down for the go of the Gospel. Go.

8

APOSTOLIC GRACE

The new breed will boast! They will gloat and boast, not in themselves, but in the Lord! They will boast not in their own achievements, but in what King Jesus has done for them. The new breed will boast in their weaknesses so the strength and grace of Jesus will abound more. Their boasting will be solely in the Lord and His grace alone!

I must go on boasting. Although there is nothing to be gained, I will go on to visions and revelations from the Lord. I know a man in Christ who fourteen years ago was caught up to the third heaven. Whether it was in the body or out of the body I do not know—God knows. And I know that this man—whether in the body or apart from the body I do not know, but God knows—was caught up to paradise and heard inexpressible things, things that no one is permitted to tell. I will boast about a man like that, but I will not boast about myself, except about my weaknesses.

Even if I should choose to boast, I would not be a fool, because I would be speaking the truth. But I refrain, so no one will think more of me than is warranted by what I do or say, or because of these surpassingly great revelations. Therefore, in order to keep me from becoming conceited, I was given a thorn in my flesh, a messenger of Satan, to torment me. Three times I pleaded with the Lord to take it away from me. But he said to me, "My grace is sufficient for you, for my power is made perfect in weakness."

Therefore I will boast all the more gladly about my weaknesses, so that Christ's power may rest on me. That is why, for Christ's sake, I delight in weaknesses, in insults, in hardships, in persecutions, in difficulties. For when I am weak, then I am strong. (2 Corinthians 12:1-10)

The Apostle Paul wasn't shying away from vulnerability. In fact, he boasted in his limited humanity. He wrote boldly and showed the Corinthian church how he was truly an apostle. Not because of his heavenly encounters and the many miracles and signs that followed him, but because of how he fully depended on the Lord for everything.

There were many super-apostles around that time who paraded their fancy teachings, shocking miracles, and personal agendas. However, Paul was not writing to the Corinthians to persuade them to believe in him, but to focus in the exaltation of the true Gospel of Jesus Christ.

TRUE APOSTLE

Paul was telling the Corinthian Church that his ministry and apostleship was true, not because of all he'd seen or experienced, but because of grace. He continued to persevere through all of it, in the supernatural grace of Jesus.

A true apostle doesn't parade himself with signs and wonders, but humbly exalts Christ, showing how deficient and lost they would be without Him. Without Jesus, what we carry is nothing. Without Jesus, a minister can walk and move in the spirit of witchcraft and power, but lack grace and the anointing of the Holy Spirit.

True apostolic ministries will point us to Jesus, not themselves. They will point the people to worship their God, not the signs and wonders. They will point the sheep to follow and hear the voice of their Shepherd, not the wolves in sheep's clothing.

The apostolic ministry is based solely on grace. We can only live by grace and we can only love by grace. It is by the grace of God that we can ever be called, continue on, or finish strong.

APOSTOLIC PERSEVERANCE

I persevered in demonstrating among you the marks of a true apostle, including signs, wonders and miracles. How were you inferior to the other churches, except that I was never a burden to you? Forgive me this wrong! (2 Corinthians 12:12-13)

The grace of Jesus anoints us to keep going. The grace of Jesus keeps us in His favor. The grace of Jesus keeps us strong and mighty; to break down barriers, walls, and barricades. The grace of Jesus anoints us to what we cannot do in our original and lowly nature. His grace anoints us to win.

Without the grace of Jesus, we wouldn't be the winners we already are. Without His grace, we wouldn't be able to conquer the enemy and possess the land. Without His grace, we wouldn't be able to be a light to the nations. Without His grace, we wouldn't be His people, His holy Bride.

Have you ever felt like giving up? I'm sure Paul wanted to throw in the towel every now and then. But he didn't! He couldn't be stopped. He was in love, and he was possessed by the Holy Spirit. Nothing could hold back the power of Jesus within him! He was unstoppable! No attack, no demon, no sickness, no trial, no tragedy, no form of political correctness, no governmental regime, no false brothers, no plague, and no venom could hold him down!

Because the grace of Jesus was fully alive in him! Nothing can hold down the grace of our God!

It is His grace that anoints us to persevere, as Jesus pressed on and moved forward, holding the weight of wrath, dying on the Cross. It was grace that sustained Him until it was finished.

Perseverance is the grace of the apostolic age. It's not about our own zeal or passion, but the grace of the Lord. The grace of the times we're living in is that we are sent in the name of Jesus—not the name of a minister, a man or woman of God, or even in the name of a ministry, church, or organization. We are sent in the name of Jesus. There is no name that is as high, authoritative, and revered as His. In all the heavens and earth, the name of Yeshua will forever be held in the highest of honor and esteem.

Jesus has sent us out in full force. The word apostle in Greek means "the sent out ones." We have been "apostolo'd" in His name. Apostolo is also combined with the Greek word, ekballo, which means "violently thrust, pushed, birthed out"! It was often used to describe a demon violently coming out of a person!

This is violence! The Lord has apostolo'd us into the world. He has sent us out; thrust us out, from the womb of His power. In the same way King Jesus rose from the grave, He has saved us and sent us out to be like sheep amongst wolves.

We are destined to win the battles. There is no losing! There is an abundance of grace because we've been sent out in His great name. There is an abundance of grace if we are in His will. There is an abundance of grace if we commit a matter to the Lord! He shall see all of our works fulfilled and established. There is an abundance of grace because King Jesus is fully responsible for seeing us, His children and ambassadors, backed up with Kingdom power. That is the power of the Father's love, grace, mercy, and compassion. There is nothing more moving and powerful than the grace of God.

Jesus came in the ministry of grace and truth. Truth without grace is Law without mercy. Truth without grace is an incomplete

Gospel. Truth without grace is an incomplete picture of Jesus, which is a false representation of the Father.

Truth without grace is what many churches have: Nothing. It is having the form of godliness but not having actual power. God didn't make us to be powerless; He created us to be powerful. Love in relationship makes us powerful. Get ready for a power activation.

We need the truth to set us free; however, we also need Jesus' grace to keep us free. It is only by grace that we can fulfill the will of our Heavenly Father. It is only by grace, not our own efforts, that His Kingdom can be established in the lives of created beings. In our own efforts, planning, and wisdom we can only achieve building the Tower of Babel. However, if we want to build the Kingdom of God, then we must build it with Him, in His grace, mercy, and truth. There is no other way. There is no compromise. We are in the business of building God's Kingdom, not our own palaces. We are in the ministry of bringing glory to God, not idolizing mere creation.

MARTIN LUTHER'S GRACE SOLAS

Much could be said about Martin Luther, but I believe he was possessed with the spirit of reformation. The true spirit of reformation is the DNA of the new breed. Centuries of religiosity, false rituals, idol worship, demonic corruption, and greedy bureaucracy had enslaved the people of Europe. The Gospel of light was tainted, locked and chained in the dungeons of agnosticism. The Dark Ages prevailed as the truth of the Gospel faded away from the people.

The Reformation began on October 31, 1517, when Martin Luther confronted the heresy of the Catholic Church, with the Ninety-Five Theses. This became The Protestant Reformation, which ultimately makes up half of the Christian faith—the other half being Catholicism.

THE MAIN DOCTRINES OF THE REFORMATION:

- Sola scriptura (By Scripture alone)
- Sola fida (By faith alone)
- Sola gratia (By grace alone)
- Solo Christo (By Christ alone)
- Soli Deo Gloria (Glory to God alone)

Too many churches have strayed away from the foundation that sparked the Protestant Reformation. Too many churches make things more complicated than Jesus ever intended. Keep it simple. Keep it holy.

The new breed is taking on a new apostolic reformation. This reformation will be consumed by the original doctrines of Martin Luther's Five Solas. In the Hebrew language, the number five represents grace! There will be a new reformation, birthed out of these five grace doctrines! This new breed will cry out, "Grace, grace, grace to the mountains!"

HIS GRACE IS ENOUGH

Paul was at the height of his ministry. He was writing to the Corinthian church of how he was having heavenly encounters, trances, and revelations. He was boasting in the true marks of an apostle. However, he pleaded with the Lord, three times, to take away from him a thorn in his flesh.

Have you ever had a thorn in your flesh, so deep and so sensitive, that it got under your skin all the time? Have you ever had a situation or a person push your button more than you could handle? Well the grace of Jesus is enough. The grace of Jesus will anoint you to handle it and He will hand you victory over it.

The Bible is unclear as to what this thorn was. It could've been his own issues of insecurity and loneliness. It could've been feeling betrayed and belittled constantly by his own Jewish brothers. It could've been consistent persecution, as people constantly ganged up against him with vehement accusation in the spirit of death and violence.

Whatever was Paul's issue, he pleaded with the Lord to take it away. The Lord responded three times that His grace was sufficient for him. This is the heart of the Gospel and all apostolic ministry. "My grace is sufficient for you!"

Whether in lack or plenty, His grace is sufficient for us. Whether alone or surrounded by people, His grace is sufficient for us. Do you believe it? Is the grace of God a reality in your life today? Do you stand alone on the cornerstone of the goodness of God?

If it wasn't for the grace of God, we would not be here. If it wasn't for the grace of God, Paul could've been consumed and overtaken by this thorn. The Lord could've instantly taken it out. He is God. Nothing is too complicated for Him. However, in His infinite wisdom, He allowed it to remain in the flesh of the greatest apostle of our Christian faith. This man, who single- handedly spread the Good News of Jesus Christ throughout the Roman empire, was dependent on the cross of grace. This man who saw miracles and revivals like no other was leaning into the cross of grace. This man who regularly had heavenly and angelic encounters was nailed into the wooden cross of grace. Nothing could stop him because nothing could stop the grace of Jesus which oozed out of him.

When life squeezes us and tests us, manifest the life and beauty of Jesus. Paul recognized how human and finite he was. He cried out for the Lord's deliverance! Instead, in His infinite wisdom, He gave him a three-fold mantle of grace.

ANOINTING OF GRACE

The grace of Jesus is what anoints us to move forward. The fact that we, whether Jew or Gentile, can be brought up and caught up into His story is because of God's grace. There was nothing about us that caused Him to be so merciful. He made a covenant with Himself to see us, the seed of Abraham, through.

God is anointing us with grace so we can endure to the end. The apostolic ministry is about perseverance. The ministry of the prophetic is about releasing hope and destiny concerning people's futures. How we endure to see that fulfilled is by the grace of the apostolic. It is in our nature to persevere. However, the Lord is giving us more than a single baptism of His Spirit; He is giving us continual in-fillings. He is giving us continual bursts of His Holy Spirit. It is essential for us to not just be filled, but to be intoxicated! To be drunk! Be drunk in His Spirit! Be drunk in the love, affections, mercy, and grace of Heaven! He wants us to be influenced by the wine of His love. This is the grace of God; the fact that the Holy Spirit can move and minister in and through people who were once sinners. Now we can be saints and be co-partners with Him in eternal exploits.

It is by grace we are called and it is by grace we can stand. The Lord has called us to be His children, to stand boldly before His throne of grace. God wants us not just to sit and not just to walk, but to be able to stand before Him, a holy God, in the uprightness of Christ.

The Lord is releasing great perseverance upon His people. Nothing can kill them, nothing can shake them, nothing can move them. The people of God are immovable and unshakable. The people of God cannot be killed because there's an immortal Lion living on the inside of them. The people of God cannot be overtaken because there's an Almighty Creator dwelling inside them. The people of God cannot lose because there's a divine risen Savior seated the inside them.

God is releasing great resilience and resistance within them; it is His Holy Spirit. It is amazing and unending grace. It is the mercies of the resurrected King. It is not the son of Joseph that we worship; it is the Son of God, the Almighty King. It is not the son of Mary that we honor; it is the Son of God incarnate. The people of God are the resistance. The people of God are the reformation. The people of God are the revival.

Our resilience in the Lord is what surprises the world. Our ongoing presence and adamant faith and action is what shocks the highest of principalities. There is no way to control a child who is fully possessed by the Spirit of their Father. There is no way in Hell that a child of Heaven can be held back.

The prison walls are coming down! The foundations are being overturned! There's a great and mighty wave of change coming and it cannot be stopped. The strong hand of God is sweeping across the earth. God is doing what He intends to do in all His glory and majesty.

APOSTOLIC GRACE

It is the grace of God that anoints us to move forward. It is not our own humanistic and logical doing. None of our greatest achievements or efforts can ever bring us to the finish line. It is only by grace that one can thoroughly build and be established upon the Cornerstone. It is the grace of God that anoints us to finish well. It was for the joy set before Jesus that He finished the race. He endured the cross and the weight of all God's wrath against sin and death for the joy of the Father. The pleasure of the Father is what cheered Him on to finish it all. It was the pleasure of the Lord that inspired and empowered Him to fulfill such a call. Without joy, it would've been impossible. Without the power of God's pleasure, the full assignment of bearing the cross would've been vain. It was the pleasure of being with the Father that gave Jesus, fully God yet fully man, the power and the ability to complete the most impossible of tasks!

ANGELS OF GRACE

Jesus went out as usual to the Mount of Olives, and his disciples followed him. On reaching the place, he said to them, "Pray that

you will not fall into temptation." He withdrew about a stone's throw beyond them, knelt down and prayed, "Father, if you are willing, take this cup from me; yet not my will, but yours be done." An angel from heaven appeared to him and strengthened him. And being in anguish, he prayed more earnestly, and his sweat was like drops of blood falling to the ground."
(Luke 22:39-44)

How do you overcome temptation? Through grace. The temptation Jesus alluded to here wasn't necessarily sin, but the temptation to fall asleep in times of urgency. His disciples needed grace to stay awake. They needed grace to be alert to see what was coming.

There is a grave temptation to fall asleep, spiritually and physically, too early. The enemy is trying to disqualify people by telling them everything is alright, tempting them to let down their hands and eyes, and to become lukewarm.

Don't give up and don't give in! Don't fall asleep! Don't be deceived and don't fall into temptation! Pray! The grace of Jesus wakes us up and keeps us on fire! The grace of Jesus keeps us strong during the watches of the night. His grace keeps us persevering into the dark hours of the night, praying and waiting for His return, no matter how hard the temptations may be.

Jesus prayed, "Father, if you are willing, take this cup from me; yet not my will, but yours be done."

The Bible says right after that, an angel from Heaven appeared and strengthened Him. There are angelic hosts coming to strengthen you. There is a company of angels coming near , to deliver you from fear.

The angels of God are showing up to strengthen you. They will accompany and assist you in fulfilling His agenda. The tangible presence of angels represents the Father's favor and grace. Much grace will be released through angelic activity.

In fact, the Bible says the angels are ascending and descending, giving and releasing gifts to all men. These angels are showing themselves to give you the gifts of His Kingdom. These are charismata, the grace gifts!

Are you ready for an abundance of grace gifts? Are you ready for an explosion and activation of the grace of God?

The God of peace will soon crush Satan under your feet. The grace of our Lord Jesus Christ be with you. (Romans 16:20)

Every good and perfect gift is from above, coming down from the Father of the heavenly lights, who does not change like shifting shadows. (James 1:17)

The Lord releases His angels to help us persevere. Without the manifest gifts of the Holy Spirit, we are not able to win. We cannot and will not accomplish all the Lord has for us without the abundance of His grace. We need all of Him and we need all of His gifts.

Jesus lived a life of surrender and operated under an open heaven because He was confident in His Father's joy. Because of the insatiable desire Jesus had to bring honor and glory to His Father, He gave up His life. Jesus saw there was greater value in bringing glory to the Father than living by His own comforts and choices and rights. He laid it all down in view of the incomparable glory of the finished work.

The power of sonship is greater than the works of slavery. The love of sonship is greater than the mandates of servanthood. The commitment of marriage is greater than the division of divorce. The willingness of surrender is greater than the yoke of arrogant independence. God is raising up a resilient army that is unmoved by the fading vanities of this world, that has the fire of God running in their veins.

This army will not be afraid. Its members will prove the very the existence of God. Their lives will exemplify the very nature of God. Their obedience will set the world ablaze and leave all people in the wonder of God.

God is anointing us to plow and plow and plow until all the grounds of the earth are plowed and there is more need for oxen. But until the world is clean and holy as the City of Zion, there is still a need to get down, dirty, and messy. Until all types of people are harvested, there is still a need for workers. Until all the nations are singing to the Lamb, there is still a need for messengers. God is raising up anointed and appointed warriors to win the battles over human souls.

GRACE BREAKS THE CHAINS

The crowd joined in the attack against Paul and Silas, and the magistrates ordered them to be stripped and beaten with rods. After they had been severely flogged, they were thrown into prison, and the jailer was commanded to guard them carefully. When he received these orders, he put them in the inner cell and fastened their feet in the stocks.

About midnight Paul and Silas were praying and singing hymns to God, and the other prisoners were listening to them. Suddenly there was such a violent earthquake that the foundations of the prison were shaken. At once all the prison doors flew open, and everyone's chains came loose. The jailer woke up, and when he saw the prison doors open, he drew his sword and was about to kill himself because he thought the prisoners had escaped. But Paul shouted, "Don't harm yourself! We are all here!" The jailer called for lights, rushed in and fell trembling before Paul and Silas. He then brought them out and asked, "Sirs, what must I do to be saved?" (Acts 16:22-30 NIV)

Prison couldn't stop these two men who were possessed by the Spirit. They were not regular, average men, but they were possessed with the power of God. They were determined not to be deterred in their devotion to the Lord.

It was their love and grace that caused them to override the factual existence of being chains, behind bars, persecuted for their faith. Death was knocking at their door. The unknown was staring straight into their eyes. Fear and terror was caving into their very consciousness. However, they did not let these facts put them into a corner.

No! They let their fiery hot praise and worship, their love for God, warm up that ice-cold prison cell. The frigid walls of the prison were nothing compared to the fire of the Holy Spirit and His passion that burned within them.

The Holy Ghost so burned within them that the prison guards' hearts were melted with fear and trembling. The angels manifested the miraculous power of God and the shook the foundations of the building! It wasn't just the doors, the walls or the ceilings. The foundations of the prison shook! God is into shaking and refurbishing the strength of our foundations.

God is not just concerned with the details of what is built on top; He is even more interested in the deep, foundational pillars of our lives. The persecution, the prison doors, the situation that they were in, could've stopped their joy, their happiness and their childlike worship of the Lord! But these natural elements were not able to snuff out the supernatural power of God. The natural has no effect on the Holy Spirit. Nothing can come between you and the blood. Nothing can come between you and the Father.

It was their praise that broke them free! Their praise activated the power of the angels. The angels coming with power was a byproduct of the extravagant flooding of praise and worship that overflowed from the hearts of Paul and Barnabas. Nothing can stop us! Nothing can stop the praise of God's people, the tribe of Judah!

That is why the people of God were known as Jews. The word "Jew" is derived from "Judah," meaning "praise, or the people of praise." God is raising up extravagant praise in this hour from the mouths of average men and women. This praise is going to break every yoke, wall, and barrier. This praise is going to break open the atmosphere. This praise is going to bring forth a great shift in our lives. Nothing is impossible for the people of praise. Nothing is impossible for those who know their God.

Praise is most potent when it is released in the valleys and the desert seasons. Worship is most true when it is done in the seasons of distance, dryness, and desolation. God is raising up a people who powerfully worship Him, no matter what the season.

Praise is the overflow of grace. Grace causes a person to worship with his or her whole heart, and exuberance and freedom.

I know what it is to be in need, and I know what it is to have plenty. I have learned the secret of being content in any and every situation, whether well fed or hungry, whether living in plenty or in want. I can do all this through him who gives me strength.
(Philippians 4:12-13 NIV)

There is a secret blessing in contentment no matter what the season. This is a grace that causes us to thrive and not just survive in every season of our lives. God wants us to continue, strong in the Lord, no matter what the situation. This is what the power of God does.

Watch God supernaturally move you through legions of demons and through the darkest of days. The bright light of God's power and love does this unconditionally and without limit .

SOLA GRATIA

The man who wrote more than half of the New Testament. The man who took the Gospel of Jesus Christ, to the highest of courts of Rome and to the furthest of routes in Europe. The man who stood face to face with Peter and rebuked him. The man who was saved on the road to Damascus as he was ordering Christians to be killed. This man, the Apostle Paul, knew that it was all about the manifest grace of Jesus Christ.

This was the Gospel that he preached and walked out: Living by grace alone. In the words of Apostle Paul:

Greet one another with a holy kiss. All God's people here send their greetings. May the grace of the Lord Jesus Christ, and the love of God, and the fellowship of the Holy Spirit be with you all.
(2 Corinthians 13:12-14)

Intimacy with one another, being in koinonia fellowship, is how we stay in the grace of Jesus and in the love of God.

May the grace of our Lord Jesus Christ be with you.
(1 Thessalonians 5:28)

The grace of our Lord Jesus Christ be with you all.
(2 Thessalonians 3:18)

The grace of the Lord Jesus Christ be with your spirit. Amen.
(Philippians 4:23)

9

THE FOURTH MAN

He said, "Look! I see four men walking around in the fire, unbound and unharmed, and the fourth looks like a son of the gods." (Daniel 4:25)

There is a fourth man appearing in the fire. Wherever you and I are gathered in His name, He is also there. There is nothing that can separate us from the love connection we have with the King of Glory. His uncreated nature is appearing in unusual ways.

Where Jesus is, there is freedom! Where Jesus is, there is victory! It doesn't matter what trials or tribulations come our way, we will be unbound and unharmed! We will freely walk around our enemies. We will be free with Emmanuel.

Jesus is the fourth man in the fire. Jesus was and still is fully God and fully man. In Hebrew, the number four represents new creation, rest, and multiplication. Jesus is the fourth man in the fire. There is new creation power in rest and multiplication when you are in the fire.

Whenever God goes before you, do not be content with a mere manifestation of miracles or with a created angelic messenger.

Only settle for the Lord Himself to go before you! God has gone before you! He is with you in every situation and every day and week of our season. He is with us in every moment, every morning, every month. Jesus was, and is, and is to come!

FRIENDS OF THE FIRE

Jesus is the fourth man in the fire. He is looking for friends who will burn with Him in love and zeal.

But there are some Jews whom you have set over the affairs of the province of Babylon—Shadrach, Meshach and Abednego— who pay no attention to you, Your Majesty. They neither serve your gods nor worship the image of gold you have set up."

Furious with rage, Nebuchadnezzar summoned Shadrach, Meshach and Abednego. So these men were brought before the king, and Nebuchadnezzar said to them, "Is it true, Shadrach, Meshach and Abednego, that you do not serve my gods or worship the image of gold I have set up? Now when you hear the sound of the horn, flute, zither, lyre, harp, pipe and all kinds of music, if you are ready to fall down and worship the image I made, very good. But if you do not worship it, you will be thrown immediately into a blazing furnace. Then what god will be able to rescue you from my hand?" (Daniel 4:12-15)

It's interesting that Daniel's three friends were tied together. Your friends shouldn't hold you down, but they should help hold you together. The people who are in your life shouldn't hold you away from the call of God, but they should be like the other spy out of the two, who wanted to go all the way in! Don't be with the other ten negative spies who gave bad reports. Be one of the chosen few, who are filled with great faith and attempt great exploits for their God, no matter what the cost.

The Lord wants us to be willing to be thrown into the furnace of affliction, together as a body. Even when our Daniels and leaders are nowhere to be found, will we choose to stick together and make the right choice?

Even when Jesus our Shepherd is taken away, will the sheep scatter and disperse? Will we stick together as one, even when the Judases betray us and the Peters are nowhere to be found? How will we respond? Will the training and examples our leaders have given us be enough when they are no longer around?

Shakings are the true tests of friendships and relationships. The true test of unity isn't in the times of prosperity and peace, but the times of tragedies and tribulations. Will we back away when times are hard, or will be stand by the ones we love when the boat is rocked by the waves and winds?

The fire of God truly reveals what is valuable. It is the fire of God that burns away the dross and the chaff and reveals the materials that won't burn away. The solid elements of our faith are what remain and ultimately matter in this lifetime.

There is a testing of unity occurring all across the earth. The devil opposes the unity of the brethren, but that gives the family of Christ the opportunity to mature and unite in love.

THE TESTS OF FIRE

Shadrach, Meshach and Abednego replied to him, "King Nebuchadnezzar, we do not need to defend ourselves before you in this matter. If we are thrown into the blazing furnace, the God we serve is able to deliver us from it, and he will deliver us from Your Majesty's hand. But even if he does not, we want you to know, Your Majesty, that we will not serve your gods or worship the image of gold you have set up."

Then Nebuchadnezzar was furious with Shadrach, Meshach and Abednego, and his attitude toward them changed. He ordered the furnace heated seven times hotter than usual and commanded some of the strongest soldiers in his army to tie up Shadrach,

Meshach and Abednego and throw them into the blazing furnace. So these men, wearing their robes, trousers, turbans and other clothes, were bound and thrown into the blazing furnace. The king's command was so urgent and the furnace so hot that the flames of the fire killed the soldiers who took up Shadrach, Meshach and Abednego, and these three men, firmly tied, fell into the blazing furnace.

Then King Nebuchadnezzar leaped to his feet in amazement and asked his advisers, "Weren't there three men that we tied up and threw into the fire?" They replied, "Certainly, Your Majesty." He said, "Look! I see four men walking around in the fire, unbound and unharmed, and the fourth looks like a son of the gods."

Nebuchadnezzar then approached the opening of the blazing furnace and shouted, "Shadrach, Meshach and Abednego, servants of the Most High God, come out! Come here!" So Shadrach, Meshach and Abednego came out of the fire, and the satraps, prefects, governors and royal advisers crowded around them. They saw that the fire had not harmed their bodies, nor was a hair of their heads singed; their robes were not scorched, and there was no smell of fire on them.

Then Nebuchadnezzar said, "Praise be to the God of Shadrach, Meshach and Abednego, who has sent his angel and rescued his servants! They trusted in him and defied the king's command and were willing to give up their lives rather than serve or worship any god except their own God. Therefore I decree that the people of any nation or language who say anything against the God of Shadrach, Meshach and Abednego be cut into pieces and their houses be turned into piles of rubble, for no other god can save in this way." Then the king promoted Shadrach, Meshach and Abednego in the province of Babylon. (Daniel 4:16-30)

The systems of the earth and the governments of the world are shaking. All the kingdoms of the world are becoming the king-doms of our God. Great kings, princes, presidents, and magistrates are turning to the Lord by the thousands. People of incredible influence and positions of power are going to be shocked by the glory of God.

The principalities of the world are waiting to see what you will do and how you will respond when times get hard. This generation is waiting to see whether you fail or miraculously succeed with all odds against you. This is the faith that we have in serving a supernatural and miraculous God. The Lord is looking for people who will not love their lives unto death (Revelation 12:11).

The Lord is planting supernatural courage and boldness in His children to withstand the pressures of the world. These seeds will blossom into the turning of many nations. The bold audacity of Daniel's three friends was shocking. It made the heads of Babylon turn and it made a demand on Heaven. It caught the attention of the Father.

The Lord cannot resist blessing and coming down Himself to intervene and lift up His people when such bold faith is enacted. This generation is teeming with people who are speaking up for their faith and saying to the principalities of the air:

"We do not need to defend ourselves before you in this matter. If we are thrown into the blazing furnace, the God we serve is able to deliver us from it, and he will deliver us from Your Majesty's hand. But even if he does not, we want you to know, Your Majesty, that we will not serve your gods or worship the image of gold you have set up."(Daniel 3:16-18)

Why bow down to worship a false god when you can be lifted up by the Lord, the God of Israel? Dying in the name of the Lord is much greater than kneeling down to the Baals of the day. There is no greater honor than being able to worship our God, no matter what the cost.

When we don't bow down to the false images of gold, then the Lord will exalt us in the true image of God.

Many people are asking who is this God we serve? Many people will travel from afar to ask questions that are impossible for mere humans to answer. We need of an answer from the Divine. We need the answers that will satisfy the secrets of the souls of men.

As King Nebuchadnezzar asked Shadrach, Meschach, and Abednego, "Is it true?"

GREAT PROMOTION

The whole world will see these great miracles! The whole world will see the ones who serve Him standing with God Himself. There is a sight to be seen! There is a wonder being revealed! There is great promotion for those who withstand the tests of fire. There is great promotion for those who do not fear the pangs of the shadow of death. There is great promotion for those who rise up, victorious, trusting in their God, no matter what the situation.

There is great Kingdom promotion but it is given only to those who can be trusted. People who willingly walk into the fires of tests will be rewarded greatly. The new breed will jump at the chance to win trophies for defeating the Goliaths of the day.

Continue to choose righteousness and seek first the Kingdom, and all things will be added unto you.
(Matthew 6:33 NIV)

As he was talking with them, Goliath, the Philistine champion from Gath, stepped out from his lines and shouted his usual defiance, and David heard it. Whenever the Israelites saw the man, they all fled from him in great fear. Now the Israelites had been saying, "Do you see how this man keeps coming out? He comes out to defy Israel. The king will give great wealth to the man who kills him. He will also give him his daughter in marriage and will exempt his family from taxes in Israel."

> David asked the men standing near him, "What will be done for the man who kills this Philistine and removes this disgrace from Israel? Who is this uncircumcised Philistine that he should defy the armies of the living God?" They repeated to him what they had been saying and told him, "This is what will be done for the man who kills him." (1 Samuel 17:23-27)

ADDED UNTO YOU

All Israel heard Goliath's mocking taunts. They heard the death threats, and the spirit of fear caused them to flee! The people of God are not to flee! We are meant to be free and to set the captives free! The warriors turned into worriers because of the lies that possessed their minds.

But while the trained warriors listened to the lies, David heard something else. He didn't hear and become fearful; he heard and become hopeful. This little shepherd boy heard and became bold.

He heard of the grand opportunity for trophies and blessings for whoever defeated this giant. He heard of the prize set aside for the one who removed this disgrace from Israel. David heard the right thing. David heard and obeyed what was in his heart.

What are you and I prone to hearing? Do we tend to hear negativity or do we hear positivity? Do we hear fear or do we hear courage and bravery? Do we hear the words of death or do we hear the words of life?

Hearing the words of God strengthens us and empowers us to move. The Word of God causes us to do the impossible, the things we cannot do in our natural state.

What will be done for the man who stands up for Jesus? Think of the harvest when a grain of wheat chooses to fall. Think of the souls of lost sons and daughters that will be returned to the Father because of the love of Jesus. Think of what the Lord can do with the life of one man or one woman.

There is great promotion for those who aren't afraid to risk it all for the sake of the Gospel. The wealth of the wicked and the riches of the nations are coming to those who put their lives in God's hands. Cities are given to those servants who learn to multiply their talents.

FOUNDATIONS OF GOLD

The Lord is into making us as pure as gold. Gold represents perfection, carries the highest value and is the most indestructible of metals. The Lord is turning us into pure, uncontaminated gold.

Those who do not bow down to Nebuchadnezzar's image will be molded into the image of God. Those who don't fall to the seductive and pervasive fear of this age will be regarded as the purest gold.

Don't fall for the counterfeit. Be real, and be the best. Don't follow all the trends, fads, and fashions of the day. Don't be another foolish sheep being led into the path of destruction. Don't be comfortable with political correctness. Do what is right and be blameless in the sight of God.

> The crucible for silver and the furnace for gold, but the LORD tests the heart. (Proverbs 17:3)

> By the grace God has given me, I laid a foundation as a wise builder, and someone else is building on it. But each one should build with care. For no one can lay any foundation other than the one already laid, which is Jesus Christ. If anyone builds on this foundation using gold, silver, costly stones, wood, hay or straw, their work will be shown for what it is, because the Day will bring it to light. It will be revealed with fire, and the fire will test the quality of each person's work. If what has been built survives, the builder will receive a reward. If it is burned up, the builder will suffer loss but yet will be saved—even though only as one escaping through the flames. (1 Corinthians 3:10-15)

God is the God of the gold! Meaning He is Lord over what is

most pure, holy, and prudent. He is Lord over the most honest measurements and issues of the heart. God is absolutely holy.

Don't measure yourself by the things that will fall away. Sow yourself into the things that are eternal. Don't burden yourself with the temporary stubble, wood, and hay, but throw yourself into what is everlasting, such as gold, silver, and costly stones. This is our inheritance. This is the foundation of Jesus, which we are being built upon.

God is into forming us into His perfect image. He doesn't expect perfection and doesn't care for religious performance, but He does expect us to be willing to be molded and refined by Him. This comes by obedience, love, and devotion to the Lord, no matter what the cost. There is no cost too great for following the voice of the Lord.

Daniel's three friends denied the government and the idolatrous antichrist spirit, and did not defile the name of God. They did not bow down to those idols, and kept their sanctity and sanity in surrendering themselves 100 percent to the Lord.

The pit of fire did not scare them. Rather their fear of the Lord caused them to boldly declare that whether He chose to save them or they burned to death, they would continue to worship the Lord, the God of Israel.

They came out of the fire victorious, new, holy and golden! They were refined in the fire. It is the purifying fire of God that perfects us. It is His holy Word that refines us. God wants us not to fear the trials, testings, and tribulations of life, but to face them boldly, with the power of the Holy Spirit. The fire inside you is greater than the fires of the world. He who is in you is greater than he who is in the world.

Because Shadrach, Meschach, and Abednego were pure in their hearts and devotion to the Lord, nothing on their bodies burned in the fire. Although the fires were turned up seven times hotter than usual, because they were already in Christ's perfection, there was no harm done to them. There was no smell of fire on them, and their tunics weren't even singed! In fact, the holiness of Christ was so great that even though they were unharmed, the soldiers guarding them died. There is judgment in the fire. There is right-eous judgment in the seven-fold, all-consuming perfection of God.

ALL-CONSUMING FIRE

For our God is a consuming fire. (Hebrew 12:29)

Jesus was the burning bush that Moses encountered in the desert. (Exodus 3:1-4)

I baptize you with water for repentance. But after me comes one who is more powerful than I, whose sandals I am not worthy to carry. He will baptize you with the Holy Spirit and fire. (Matthew 3:11)

John the Baptist — the preparer of the way, the Elijah of the day — prophesied about the One who would baptize with Holy Spirit and fire! Jesus Christ wants to baptize us in His Holy Spirit and fire! Not only is He washing and sanctifying us on the outside, but He is cleansing and refining our beings from the inside.

The Lord is releasing the baptism of fire to destroy the works of the enemy. The Lord is releasing a fresh baptism of fire that will genuinely transform us. The baptism of fire is the baptism of Heaven, which changes us from the inside out.

The baptism of water is the public statement of owning Christ's death and resurrection. It is the public account of becoming a born-again, new creation with Christ Jesus, our risen Savior. The baptism of water is definitely a doctrinally important part of being a true disciple. However, the baptism of the Holy Spirit and fire is even more important.

Sadly, the baptism of water has become more of a traditional, religious duty than a personal, powerful, joyful declaration! Sadly, the baptism of water has been treated as a tradition of denomina-tions, rather than a supernatural sign of being born again.

The many years of calling people in the baptism of water was meant to prepare us for the baptism of the Holy Spirit and fire. The all-consuming fire of God cannot be controlled but will overtake a person inside and out.

MESSENGERS OF FIRE

The Bible says there are seraphim around the sapphire throne of God. In Hebrew, serah means "fire." These seraphim are angelic, celestial beings, which are on fire because they minister near the throne of God. The seraphim do not burn out because they are burning with the flame of God's rule.

Above him were seraphim, each with six wings: With two wings they covered their faces, with two they covered their feet, and with two they were flying. (Isaiah 6:2)

In speaking of the angels he says, "He makes his angels spirits, and his servants flames of fire." (Hebrews 1:7)

The angels of God are His burning ones. His angelic messengers are on fire. Those who come around us will catch the fire. Those who come near us will feel the heat of the fire of God. All impurities and indecencies and infirmities will burn off. The power of God's heat and fiery love will melt and burn away all inferior substances.

God is into perfection. He is into us being as perfect as He is. However, our time here on earth is the time of purification. He expects us to be like Daniel's friends and walk out of the fire untouched, unburned, without marks, scars, blisters, or bruises. God wants us to walk out of the fires of life looking like Him!

Gold is the most precious and expensive type of metal. Royalty and the financial systems of the world valued this metal like none other. Gold is scientifically proven to be the least reactive element: It does not react in conditions of fire, wind, raging waters, or any other type of phenomena. Gold is the most malleable metal, and resists the effects of most acids. Gold is longer-lasting and more durable than any other metal. Of all other earthly metals, gold is the champion.

The Bible says wisdom is to be sought more fervently than gold. The fire cannot destroy its elements. The fire will only test it and reveal the fake and the false, so that only the truth remains. No fakery can withstand the fire of God.

God wants us to be bright and shining, in our purest form. That looks like walking out our sonship in Christ Jesus. The Church, being the pure Bride of Christ, emanates the image of Christ Himself. It has no defilement, depravity, weakness, or lowliness. It looks like the complete Gospel of Jesus Christ.

The cultures of the world cannot water down the Gospel. The spirit of this age cannot manipulate the gold of our true image in Christ. The trials and tribulations of this fallen world cannot and will not deform the true value of knowing God. Nothing can destroy the gold of our faith.

SEVEN TIMES HOTTER!

Then Nebuchadnezzar was furious with Shadrach, Meshach and Abednego, and his attitude toward them changed. He ordered the furnace heated seven times hotter than usual (Daniel 4:16)

God is turning us into gold. The Bible is a long story of the faithfulness of our forever-loving and everlasting God. The Bible is a compiled witness to the God who never leaves us or forsakes us. The Lord does not leave us to burn and die in persecution. He is right there with us in the fires of life! The Lord is the fourth man in the fire.

The world will see the Lord whenever we choose to step into the fire. The fire is our home, the habitat in which our hearts are revealed. How we respond in times of crisis or victory reveals our character. The world is waiting to see the character of Christ manifest through our lives.

The Hebrew number seven represents perfection and completion. The Lord is releasing His seventh day upon us. The seventh day, as recorded in the Bible, stands for the Sabbath. The Lord of the Sabbath is perfecting us by His grace, mercy, and rest! It is His will that we rest in Him during the times of testing.

It is His will that we rest in the Lord of the Sabbath through every situation of our lives. That is how we will be perfected. That is how we will be like gold! We will walk out the perfect nature of Christ when we walk out the purified, holy nature cultivated in the times of being with our Lord and Savior.

We are perfected like gold, not when work and do many things in Jesus' name, but when we choose to rest with Him and in Him. The shalom of God is what causes us to be truly purified. Human beings are not perfected without the rest of the Holy Spirit. It is fit for a king and a lord to rest on his throne. It is rightly fitting for a son or daughter of God to be seated with Him in the heavenly places, not moved by every wicked wind that blows.

Honoring the sabbath is one of the main ways we can stay in tune with the Divine. The sabbath manifests the seventh-day anointing. The sabbath manifests the perfection of God. The sabbath is a time and space set apart to allow the Holy Spirit to properly search the heart to reveal what is gold and what is not. We allow the Holy Spirit to search our ins and outs. This is the only way we will be perfected.

A life filled with grace looks like Jesus. A life filled with works looks like a dead man. Labor is part of the fallen nature, the curse which infected creation that Adam and Eve left behind. But living in abundant grace looks like the Garden of Eden. There's no strife, no striving; there's no stress, no sweat or toil. It is easy, fun, and filled with grace. That is what walking in intimacy with Jesus is like: Being with Him in the cool of the day.

———

FROM SILVER TO GOLD

The Lord's been speaking to me about gold for the last several months. A while ago, I wrote a prophetic blog titled "Silver to Gold," after the Lord told me He was turning my silver into gold.

On my twenty-fifth birthday, the Lord began to speak to me about the meaning of silver. Twenty-five is the silver jubilee. The Lord gave me a cool signet ring, which was titanium (silver-colored) with a blue opal, signifying the season He was bringing me into.

On the day of my celebration, one of my dear spiritual fathers, Prophet Gershom Sikaala, gave me his silver-coated lion necklace. As he was praying over me, he took off the necklace and put it on me. I was overly blessed as this special gift from my father prophetically confirmed what the Lord was speaking to me and doing.

About a month later, I was in Tijuana, Mexico, for our church's quarterly mission trip. There were many signs, wonders, and miracles, and as always, the people and church of God were greatly edified. Around that time, one of my spiritual mothers, Apostle Marisela Padilla, asked me to minister at her church, for a late Friday-night prayer vigil. I was physically tired, but out of love and honor, I went right after ministering at Selah, the House of Prayer in Revolucion, the city's red-light district.

I shared my heart about faith and finances. Afterward Mama Marisela gave me her gold Jesus-fish necklace. It was a very special item she had worn for nearly seventeen years, through many seasons of her life, everywhere she went. She told me she felt led to bless me with it, as she loved me as her own son! I was enthralled by the faithfulness of our God, humbled by Mama Marisela's generosity, and amazed at seeing this word come to pass.

Last December, I was in Dubai, where the best gold in the world is found. Months before that, I had given my precious signet ring away and since then, the desire to get a new one was deep in my heart. I searched for the right one in Dubai for two days. I was confident the Lord wanted to bless me with this special gift, prophetically signifying the great new season I was entering. I didn't found one before I had to go back to Los Angeles—but I felt the Lord speak tell me not worry because He was going to bless me.

The next day at our home church, Prophet Vincent Zavala stopped his preaching and called me up front. All night long, I had been noticing a large ring on his right hand. He said that for the last three days, the Lord had been telling him to give that ring away! He then shared that he hadn't worn it for five years; it had been tucked away in a drawer. He intended it to be a special inheritance he was going to pass on to his eldest son—but now he knew I was the one he was supposed to give it to!

Wow, God is faithful! After leaving Dubai a bit sad, without a ring on my hand, the very next day, the Lord surprised me! The ring is made of platinum and eighteen-carat white gold, with six blue diamonds! Diamonds are forever! The Lord once again astounded me with His prophetic word, saying He was turning all my silver into gold!

These stories are about more than jewelry, though. They display the prophetic nature of God's story! I know all of this prophetically confirms my maturity in the Lord. Truly, He's turning all our silver into gold.

The Lord is into purity, perfection, and maturity. He is into us being the Bride without flaw, blemish, or wrinkle. He is into us being the Bride that is holy, beautiful, and equal to Christ Himself. We are His Bride. We are with Him in the fire. He is turning all of our mourning into dancing and all our weeping into joy. He is turning all our silver into gold. He is purifying and refining all our being into His perfect nature. As Austin Powers said in the movie Goldmember, "I love gold!"

Well, so does the Lord! Are you a gold member? The new breed will be made up of people who love and live through the fire of God. They will accept the tests that come and victoriously walk out of the furnace as the pure and perfected Bride of Christ.

10

THE GLORY REALM

And we all, who with unveiled faces contemplate the Lord's glory, are being transformed into his image with ever-increasing glory, which comes from the Lord, who is the Spirit. (2 Corinthians 3:18)

There is a realm of glory from which the children of God are birthed. All the world can experience it when they encounter us. There is a realm of the supernatural that is the bread of Israel's children. This realm of glory is breaking out through Christ in us.

Creative miracles are the norm for the new breed because they've tapped into the creative nature of Christ Jesus within them. Jesus loves to create situations of hope, life, and love. Jesus is the giver of life and the builder of hope.

The new breed will move in gifts, signs and wonders. They desire to see the impossible manifested. They love to see something brilliant come out of nothing. They love to see life produced. They love seeing things coming to life and taking on flesh! They love seeing creation fully live.

It's because they love life! Creating is in their DNA, part of their God-given nature. It's who they are. If they don't create, they don't live. If they don't create, they feel like they're missing out. If they don't create, they feel dead inside. Creating with God is what they were made for; it's how they get their drive, what moves them.

OPEN HEAVENS

There is an open heaven over, above, and in every believer because Jesus is Jacob's ladder. There is an open heaven because Jesus tore the veil of division between Heaven and earth, and He has risen to the highest of heavens and is now seated at the right hand of God.

The pathway that Jesus took did not close up. It is open and will always be. This open heaven is only growing. This is the pathway where the angels of God are ascending and descending upon the earth.

He had a dream, and behold, a ladder was set on the earth with its top reaching to heaven; and behold, the angels of God were ascending and descending on it. (Genesis 28:12)

He then added, "Very truly I tell you, you will see 'heaven open, and the angels of God ascending and descending on' the Son of Man." (John 1:51)

This is how the angels of Heaven are bringing gifts to all men, through the commissioning of Jesus Christ; from His Word, sent from His throne. The angels are deploying and depositing many gifts, miracles, and packages for His holy people. These angels are ascending, carrying the incense of praise, worship, and adoration to the throne of God. They are carrying our petitions, supplications, prayers to the throne of God.

This is not merely a metaphor; it is a reality, happening now in the Spirit and in the heavenlies. These angels are releasing great miracles to the sons of men. These angels are releasing things of

Heaven and manifesting them in the place of earth. They are bringing pieces of the Kingdom of Heaven and seeing it manifest as the Kingdom of God. The Kingdom is manifesting as the realm of glory is being transferred, up and down this ladder.

THE GLORY REALM

The uncreated nature of God is His glory. The King of glory is bringing His people into this place of infinite glory, the atmosphere of Heaven. The vortex of transference is where the utmost pleasures of our God's goodness slip through the veil and touch mankind. Earth is kissed with heavenly delight when the realm of God's pleasure tangibly coming upon and into the lives of men and women.

The glory of His goodness is everywhere, and glimpses of Heaven will begin glittering and flickering here and there, until, ultimately there is no more occasional and temporary just the eternal. There will be no more death, but only the fullness of life engulfing all that is known and seen in this mortal realm.

The realm of eternity, where time, space, and matter no longer exist, is invading us. The glory is where the science of man is defied. It is where the laws of physics are dominated by the eternal laws of the Spirit and God's glory is breaking in. Heaven is truly invading earth.

The Bible lists many ways God has done, is doing and will do this, listed below.

1) THE GLORY CLOUD

And Moses was not able to enter the tent of meeting because the cloud settled on it, and the glory of the Lord filled the tabernacle. (Exodus 40:35)

And the glory of the Lord went up from the cherub to the threshold of the house, and the house was filled with the cloud,

and the court was filled with the brightness of the glory of the Lord. (Ezekiel 10:4)

In Old Testament times, the cloud of glory regularly came to fill the temple. I believe there was a tangible substance to His glory. The heavy kavod of God's glory looked like something. It felt like something. It was something. The literal weight of all that God is was experienced by those in the temple.

They would leave in awe and wonder. They would leave changed. The cloud descending gave the priests the opportunity to step into a miraculous atmosphere so pervasive even their descendants would be forever changed. To step into the realm of God's glory and the unseen world was a privilege. Stepping into a realm of wonder is what we were created to do.

There was provision, protection, and power in the appearance of the cloud. Whoever was under it or around it felt a different atmosphere. The cloud of glory became Israel's covering. It became their life source. It became their protection. Without it, there was no supernatural protection from the harsh elements of the desert. Without the cloud of glory, the Israelites would not have made it out of the wilderness alive!

Even with such miraculous and wondrous manifestations, a whole generation fell away, not allowing God's goodness to penetrate the depths of their stone-cold hearts. They did not fully receive the goodness of their God into the very fabric of their lives. Instead, they chose to follow their evil ways and worship a man-made golden calf. They tried to create a god, made in the image of a fallen animal, rather than worshipping YWH, the Creator of the universe, in Whose image they were made.

2) JESUS' SECOND COMING

Then they will see THE SON OF MAN COMING IN A CLOUD with power and great glory. (Luke 21:27, emphasis added)

And then the sign of the Son of Man will appear in the sky, and then all the tribes of the earth will mourn, and they will see the SON OF MAN COMING ON THE CLOUDS OF THE SKY with power and great glory. (Matthew 24:30, emphasis added)

Is there a purpose in stating that Jesus' return is accompanied by clouds? Is this just prophetic, Hebraic symbology? Is it just a metaphor, or is it literal? Is there a connection between Jesus' return and the biblical accounts of God's cloud of glory recorded throughout history? Is this just a coincidence or is God trying to tell us something?

The glory of the Lord is tied with the cloud. There is something unique and supernatural about it. Jesus' second coming, His return of glory and judgment, is tied to the uncreated glory realm, breaking in from perfection and eternity into our world. His glory will ultimately judge all that is fallen and will create new life. Whatever your doctrine might be, there will be a new Heaven and a new earth. There will be a new Jerusalem. This will all be created from the glory of our Creator.

As the cloud of glory descended upon the temple and the people of God during their wanderings, the cloud of glory will again descend upon God's people, with Jesus riding on top of it. The Lord will return in all His splendor, riding on the clouds with a trumpet sound!

3) SUPERNATURAL WEATHER

After an all-night march from Gilgal, Joshua took them by surprise. The Lord threw them into confusion before Israel, so Joshua and the Israelites defeated them completely at Gibeon. Israel pursued them along the road going up to Beth Horon and cut them down all the way to Azekah and Makkedah. As they fled before Israel on the road down from Beth Horon to Azekah, the Lord hurled large hailstones down on them, and more of them died from the hail than were killed by the swords of the Israelites.

On the day the Lord gave the Amorites over to Israel, Joshua said to the Lord in the presence of Israel: "Sun, stand still over Gibeon, and you, moon, over the Valley of Aijalon." So the sun stood still, and the moon stopped, till the nation avenged itself on its enemies, as it is written in the Book of Jashar.

The sun stopped in the middle of the sky and delayed going down about a full day. There has never been a day like it before or since, a day when the Lord listened to a human being. Surely the Lord was fighting for Israel! (Joshua 10:9-14)

Joshua stopped the sun and the moon. This is the glory. The Lord hurled hailstones from Heaven! Through these unusual weather changes and control, the enemies of Israel were defeated. God works in unusual ways to give His people great victory.

4) SUPERNATURAL FOOD

Jesus multiplied food. This is the glory manifesting. Famines, pestilence, disasters, and lack are nothing compared to the glory. The glory of God changes all things.

While Aaron was speaking to the whole Israelite community, they looked toward the desert, and there was the glory of the Lord appearing in the cloud. The Lord said to Moses, "I have heard the grumbling of the Israelites. Tell them, 'At twilight you will eat meat, and in the morning you will be filled with bread. Then you will know that I am the Lord your God.'" That evening quail came and covered the camp, and in the morning there was a layer of dew around the camp. When the dew was gone, thin flakes like frost on the ground appeared on the desert floor. When the Israelites saw it, they said to each other, "What is it?" For they did not know what it was. Moses said to them, "It is the bread the Lord has given you to eat. This is what the Lord has commanded: 'Everyone is to gather as much as they need. Take

an omer for each person you have in your tent.' " (Exodus 16:10-16)

Manna and quail fell from Heaven daily. This is the glory. The Bible says everyone gathered as much as they needed. Doesn't that sound familiar?

Another of his disciples, Andrew, Simon Peter's brother, spoke up, "Here is a boy with five small barley loaves and two small fish, but how far will they go among so many?"

Jesus said, "Have the people sit down." There was plenty of grass in that place, and they sat down (about five thousand men were there). Jesus then took the loaves, gave thanks, and distributed to those who were seated as much as they wanted. He did the same with the fish. (John 6:8-11) Once again, the people Jesus fed had as much as they wanted! This passage says there were twelve baskets left over!

The Lord is into showing off glimpses of His glory in and through His people. Nothing is impossible. Nothing is out of reach for the Creator who's seated inside your spirit.

5) SUPERNATURAL SPEECH

Early in the morning, as Jesus was on his way back to the city, he was hungry. Seeing a fig tree by the road, he went up to it but found nothing on it except leaves. Then he said to it, "May you never bear fruit again!" Immediately the tree withered. (Matthew 21:18-19)

Jesus commanded the fig tree to die. What could've taken a long time happened instantly. There are things that ordinarily take time, but when we operate in the glory, they will happen instantaneously, in the blink of an eye!

Life and death are in the power of the tongue. As the Lord spoke the worlds into being, so can we. Speak from the realm of His glory. Speak like the Creator, the King of glory!

6) UNUSUAL MIRACLES

Recently, our church experienced twenty-one days of revival, during which there was an outbreak of unusual miracles. These manifestations could only be explained by the glory of God breaking out among us. We didn't need to try to explain what was happening, we just experienced Him. We all experienced the Lord in different ways—heavenly visitations, dreams, and encounters. The supernatural was genuinely breaking out in a way I hadn't experienced before.

We've seen the dead raised; we've seen cancer defeated; we've seen multitudes of healings and I have witnessed countless other types of miracles with my own eyes. But what the Lord began manifesting during the twenty-one days of revival was incredible!

Some of the miracles or manifestations listed below may offend you—or they may spark a deeper hunger within you. Whatever your initial thoughts may be, I encourage you to be prayerful in the Spirit. Read your Bible and talk with the Lord about all that has been written in this book. I encourage you to stay hungry and open to the Lord, as God's ways are higher than ours and He tends to do things that are hidden in parables and often mysterious.

Multiple witnesses can testify of these sightings and experiences:

Gold Dust

For days at a time, gold dust appeared on chairs, the floor, people's hands, faces, arms, and Bibles. Sometimes it looked like flaky dust, and sometimes more solid glitter-like dots. This manifestation then began appearing in the homes of those attending the meetings.

One night, I was up until 4 a.m., texting a friend about what was happening. She then checked her arms and body and found massive amounts of gold dust covering her! I posted about it on

Facebook, and people all around the world began messaging me, telling me that they were getting it too!

The LORD their God will save his people on that day as a shepherd saves his flock. They will sparkle in his land like jewels in a crown. (Zechariah 9:16)

Supernatural Oil

When the first reports of oil manifesting in the palms of people's hands began circulating, I didn't take it too seriously. But a few days later we heard the same report from a man who had been skeptical about it until he saw it manifest out of his hands in his more conservative church on a Sunday morning. Then several other people at his church began to get it, along with the gold-dust manifestation.

Dreams and Visions

The realm of dreams was opening up during those days like I'd never seen before. A man from Ventura who shared a dream he had on the second day of this revival. He said he had a white piece of paper. It was plain and simple on the front, but the back was covered in gold dust!

A friend in Vancouver, Canada, who was watching our livestream on Facebook, reported dreaming that she was in her bedroom when chunks of gold began raining in it! The things the Spirit is doing are transferrable. Catch it!

Gemstones

"I will greatly rejoice in the LORD, my soul shall be joyful in my God; for he hath clothed me with the garments of salvation, he hath covered me with the robe of righteousness, as a bridegroom decketh himself with ornaments, and as a bride adorneth herself with her jewels." (Isaiah 61:10)

A friend of ours, whom we consider to be a prophet, experienced supernatural gemstones, pearls, and diamonds manifesting in his home for nearly a year.

I have been to his home many times. It's a simple clean place; he and his wife are the parents of young children, and they don't have the means to buy gemstones to set up a hoax so elaborate. It is a miracle.

He began passing out these gemstones in our meetings as he felt led. A woman who came consistently took the diamond he gave her to a gemologist, who certified that it was real.

These gemstones have been manifesting in our church for months now, on and off as there are seasons of increase. Members have found them in the parking lot, in their cars, in public restaurants, and other random places. God is not limited to manifesting His miracles in a church setting. The world is the perfect setting for His marvelous works.

Feathers

What do feathers have to do with God? Feathers are a common manifestation of the angelic realm. They have been popping up around certain people's homes from the church for quite a while now. Some people from another church who came for our meetings started finding feathers at their own church afterward. They knew it was supernatural as these churches were not Charismatic and didn't believe in the gifts of the Spirit.

He will cover you with His pinions, and under His wings you may seek refuge; His faithfulness is a shield and bulwark. (Psalm 91:4)

These are the creative miracles that have come forth from God's glory at His Way Life. I also have heard of reports of gold teeth miraculously appearing in people's mouths, new organs appearing in people's bodies, tumors dissolving, and new body parts and limbs growing instantaneously, financial miracles and debt cancellations, different items appearing out of thin air, and metal plates, screws, and other mechanical parts in people's bodies dissolving. I have personally witnessed many of these types of miracles myself!

There is realm of glory that is not common to man, but which is not far from our reach. The Lord wants to manifest Himself if we let Him. But it won't happen by repeating the same-old, same-old. There must be a hunger. There must be a desire. There must be genuine worship.

These signs and wonders make us one with God. It is necessary for this move of God. These types of miracles will be commonplace amongst the new breed.

THE GENERATION OF GLORY

Creative miracles will happen more and more in the days to come. They will be common. The Spirit will dominate the natural. What normally takes years to heal, build or do will be done instantly. The power to co-create with Him will become evident and instantaneous. What seems to be acceleration to our human minds is actually the layer of time vanishing. The film of time is under the command of God's heavenly children.

God set Adam in the environment of His glory at creation. Adam was brought forth into a timeless, ageless, eternal realm. There was no death, there was no sickness, there was no sin. Think about it. The Bible says God created man and woman in His image—the image of glory.

So God created mankind in his own image, in the image of God he created them; male and female he created them.
(Genesis 1:27)

If that was the DNA of the first Adam, how much more like that are we whose DNA comes from the Second Adam? Not only is God bringing us back to this nature, but He has birthed us into an even greater recreated nature.

Lack and limitations, hindrances and death began to cloud creation as sin entered. But all that was put to an end at the Cross. All these elements of the fallen nature no longer exist for the man who has given himself to the Lord. The curse is broken and the blessings of God are flooding the earth!

Man was not designed to be sick, limited, or separated from God and die. We were created to live in the glory of God, where the infinity of life breaks the barriers of time.

God spoke and created the world. God spoke and things happened. There were no limitations and no restrictions. We have been made and sent out of the all of God!

God said to Moses, "I AM WHO I AM. This is what you are to say to the Israelites: 'I AM has sent me to you.' " (Exodus 3:14)

The reason why we don't see very many miracles is because of the lack of God's glory. We have it but we need to manifest it. We have it, but the Lord wants us to know how to release it and to carry His glory wherever we go.

Worship and obedience is the stewardship of God's glory. Submission and surrender is the path to seeing God's glory be manifested.

HOLY COMMUNION

This is why we ultimately must commune with the Lord. Being in communion with Him is neither a duty nor a religious task. It is not about continuing tradition or appeasing a totalitarian god. Communion is the great privilege we have to become fully one with Him. This is the full culmination of love; becoming one! Becoming one in Spirit, so that separation becomes impossible.

The Lord wanted Adam to eat of the right tree—the tree of

life. They were to eat, drink, breathe, and soak in all of God's glory in the Garden. They were in communion with God.

When we choose to eat of Him and eat with Him, we flourish. Dominion is produced from communion. The Lord wants us manifest our true transfigured glory by the light we take in from Him.

That is why the Lord wants us to eat of Him and drink of Him, daily. It is essential not only to eat the manna, but also to drink of His blood.

"I am the bread of life. Your ancestors ate the manna in the wilderness, yet they died. But here is the bread that comes down from heaven, which anyone may eat and not die. I am the living bread that came down from heaven. Whoever eats this bread will live forever. This bread is my flesh, which I will give for the life of the world."

Then the Jews began to argue sharply among themselves, "How can this man give us his flesh to eat?" Jesus said to them, "Very truly I tell you, unless you eat the flesh of the Son of Man and drink his blood, you have no life in you. Whoever eats my flesh and drinks my blood has eternal life, and I will raise them up at the last day.

For my flesh is real food and my blood is real drink. Whoever eats my flesh and drinks my blood remains in me, and I in them. Just as the living Father sent me and I live because of the Father, so the one who feeds on me will live because of me. This is the bread that came down from heaven. Your ancestors ate manna and died, but whoever feeds on this bread will live forever."
(John 6:48-58)

The difference between believers and unbelievers is obvious. The Spirit in us brings life. The newness inside us comes from what we daily eat and meditate on.

When we eat and drink of the sacrifice of the Lamb of God,

we return to our true nature, greater than it was in the Garden. There is great glory for those who daily commune with the Lord. Do you want to avoid death? Taste and see that the Lord is good! Taste the food and drink of eternity by communing with the King of glory. Let the realm of eternity bubble up and manifest and mature out of you as you gulp down and chew up the very essence and glorious DNA of our Creator. Really, the Lord is restoring the awe and wonder of God. We must live in the awe and all of God.

THE END-TIMES LANGUAGE

And afterward, I will pour out my Spirit on all people. Your sons and daughters will prophesy, your old men will dream dreams, your young men will see visions. (Joel 2:28)

The language of God is dreams, visions, and prophecy. The End Times Army will be fully immersed in the ways God communicates. This move of God pivots on the revelation of God communicating His endless love to this world.

God is pouring out His Spirit and speaking through prophecy, dreams, and visions. Catch the wave of His Spirit. Catch the wave of His outpouring. This is the three-chord sound of the new breed that is emerging on the earth.

The signs, the wonders, the miracles, the glory; all are attributes of the goodness of our Father, reaching out in longing for love and relationship with His children. All of this is because of His love for us. All of this is because He is longing for His Bride to be fully with Him.

THE GATES OF THE SOUL

Humans are made up of three parts: spirit, soul, and body. The spirit is our inner man, the soul is our core, and the body is our shell. Those who are born-again have their spirits renewed in the Holy Spirit, therefore, causing change in the soul and body.

The human soul has three parts: the mind (logos, logic, reasoning), will (thymos, passion, spiritedness), and emotion (eros, desire, appetite).

The Lord is healing, cleansing and protecting our soul gates: The eye gate, the ear gate, the feel gate, the taste gate, and the smell gate. All of these gates to our soul can be tainted, abused, and dirtied by the devious ways of the world.

These five senses, or these gates of our soul, cause us to have certain perceptions or views of the situations we encounter. How we perceive a thing is how we will receive it and react or respond to it. The Lord wants to heal, cleanse, and protect all of the gates of our soul. The Eye/Sight Gate.

"Blessed are the pure in heart, for they will see God."
(Matthew 5:8)

It is essential for us to guard our eye gates in this generation. Salacious advertisements have possessed the eyes of our soul. Social media has corrupted and even spiritually raped the vision of our minds. The Lord wants to cleanse us from any and all impurities.

The clearer our vision, the greater Christ's light shines through us. We live to have Jesus shine through our eye gates. Love is meant to beam through the gates of our eyes.

THE MOUTH/TASTE GATE

"Woe to me!" I cried. "I am ruined! For I am a man of unclean lips, and I live among a people of unclean lips, and my eyes have seen the King, the Lord Almighty." Then one of the seraphim flew to me with a live coal in his hand, which he had taken with tongs from the altar. With it he touched my mouth and said, "See, this has touched your lips; your guilt is taken away and your sin atoned for." (Isaiah 6:5-7)

The Lord commissions Isaiah to speak His Word. Isaiah becomes a prophet of the Lord through a prophetic encounter. The Lord commissioned an angel to burn Isaiah's mouth and lips, allowing him to become a prophetic mouthpiece.

We may come from a people of unclean lips, but that doesn't need to be our identity. We may be people who used to swear like the fishermen of Galilee, but that doesn't have to be how we continue to speak.

The Lord wants to anoint our mouths so we will eat good fruit from them. The Lord is anointing our mouths so that the things we say will be holy and of Him. That is the whole concept that is behind a "kosher" lifestyle.

THE TOUCH/FEEL GATE

I have a very good friend from another country who came to visit me in Los Angeles a while ago. Whenever I would place my hand on his shoulder or press lightly against him, he would jump and shriek. He would get very uncomfortable and even scream. I thought he was just being overactive.

However, this continued for several days. As I was driving him to the airport to go home, I began to pray over him and prophesy that the Lord was going to heal him in the area of touch. I told him the Lord was going to restore the realm of physical touch in his life.

He then shared with me how his family's housekeeper had molested him as a child when his parents were not around. This was something I had discerned in the Spirit. My heart felt for him and sympathized with him as he shared this vulnerable memory. So then what happened? Has he been healed?

I believe the Father is in the business of healing and redeeming the area of touch in our lives. The brain produces different chemicals in the body through touch.

Many churches have become legalistic and religious in this area, for obvious reasons. If you are a male, you cannot sit alone with a woman. If you are a minister, you cannot be alone with the opposite gender. You can only give sideways hugs, etc. These protocols are totally understandable and absolutely wise for legal reasons.

But at the same time, how many of us need to be healed in the area of touch? How many of us have been physically or sexually abused? How many of us fear any physical interaction with another person? How does the Father view such things?

The Lord wants to heal this generation in the sense of touch and feeling. As the Lord heals all memories of abuse, He will remove negative reactions and restore healthy chemicals in the body.

I have seen the power of love in touch move and melt peoples' hearts often. In Mexico, we would hug random people, left and right. It didn't matter who they were; whether they were homeless people, working in a restaurant, or even random youth who passed by, we would rambunctiously love the people around us and hug Jesus into them.

There have been so many cases of a simple heartfelt hug, with no other agenda than sharing the Father's love, completely setting people free and healing them in many ways. The Father's love sets us free from captivity.

Many people are just a hug away from receiving Jesus. Many people are just a handshake away, a pat on the back away, a simple conversation away from Jesus! Be like Jesus and stop to give the Samaritan woman a drink. Be like Jesus and stop for the one.

HOLY SOUL GATES

The innocence of a child's love is contagious. Be a child of God today and see how powerful simple acts of love can be. Simple acts of kindness can change the world. The Lord is healing and restoring people's touch gates. Even now, I can sense the Lord setting people free from different traumas and areas of abuse. You're beautiful and your body is holy.

Touch is holy. Eating is holy. Smell is holy. Seeing is holy. Hearing is holy. Experiencing all of Jesus and the fullness of life through every single one of our soul gates is holy. These soul gates connect our spirits with the Holy Spirit. Experiencing God and all of life through the restoration of all these gates is holy, holy, holy unto the Lord.

The King of Glory is restoring our innocence and purity so we can walk out our original design, which knows no fear, abuse, hatred, anger, sickness, or death. Our original design is being restored through the love and glory of God.

Holiness is key to what the Lord is doing. To be holy means to be set apart. Jesus wants us to be holy, not common. The Holy Spirit is what distinguishes us from the common. Be set apart, having a different spirit.

We can fully feel, hear, taste, touch, smell, and experience the Kingdom in the Holy Spirit. Wherever His Holy Spirit is present, we find the Kingdom.

The new breed will live in the Holy Spirit. The new breed will live in the glory. The new breed will be all that Jesus has made them to be, walking in the realm of glory that has yet to be seen. The Lord is bringing us back to our true covenant nature that is like Him—fully eternal and everlasting.

The new breed is the generation of glory. The new breed will see the glory of God break into their midst like no other generation has seen! Get ready.

This new breed consists of you and me. There is a new breed rising.

ABOUT THE AUTHOR

Ben Lim is the Senior Pastor of His Way Life, in the heart of Kore-atown, Los Angeles. He is a dynamic Millennial preacher who has traveled to over thirty nations in just the last decade. He spent his earlier years in the mission fields of Asia and Southeast Asia, preaching the Gospel to unreached people groups.

He is the CEO of Ben Lim TV and Ben Lim Ministries. His ministry is accompanied with notable signs, wonders, and miracles. He has ministered in evangelistic crusades in Pakistan, Dubai, and Africa seeing hundreds of thousands come to Jesus! He is ordained by Pastor Benny Hinn and the WHF (World Healing Fellowship) and is a trusted voice and a regular feature on the Elijah List and many other prophetic channels.

Visit Ben's Website at:

www.benlimglobal.com

ALSO FROM BEN:

Men of Valor (2016)

"*Men of Valor* has the potential to be one of those hallmark books that shapes a whole generation and releases a mighty revival among men in the earth..." — **Corey Russell**

Glory Impartations Soaking EP

PRODUCTS AVAILABLE FOR PURCHASE AT:

BENLIMGLOBAL.COM | CDBABY.COM | AMAZON.COM

PULPIT TO PAGE PUBLISHING CO. BOOKS MAY BE ORDERED
THROUGH BOOKSELLERS OR BY CONTACTING:
PULPIT TO PAGE ‖ U.S.A & ABROAD
PULPITTOPAGE.COM

Made in the USA
Middletown, DE
06 March 2019